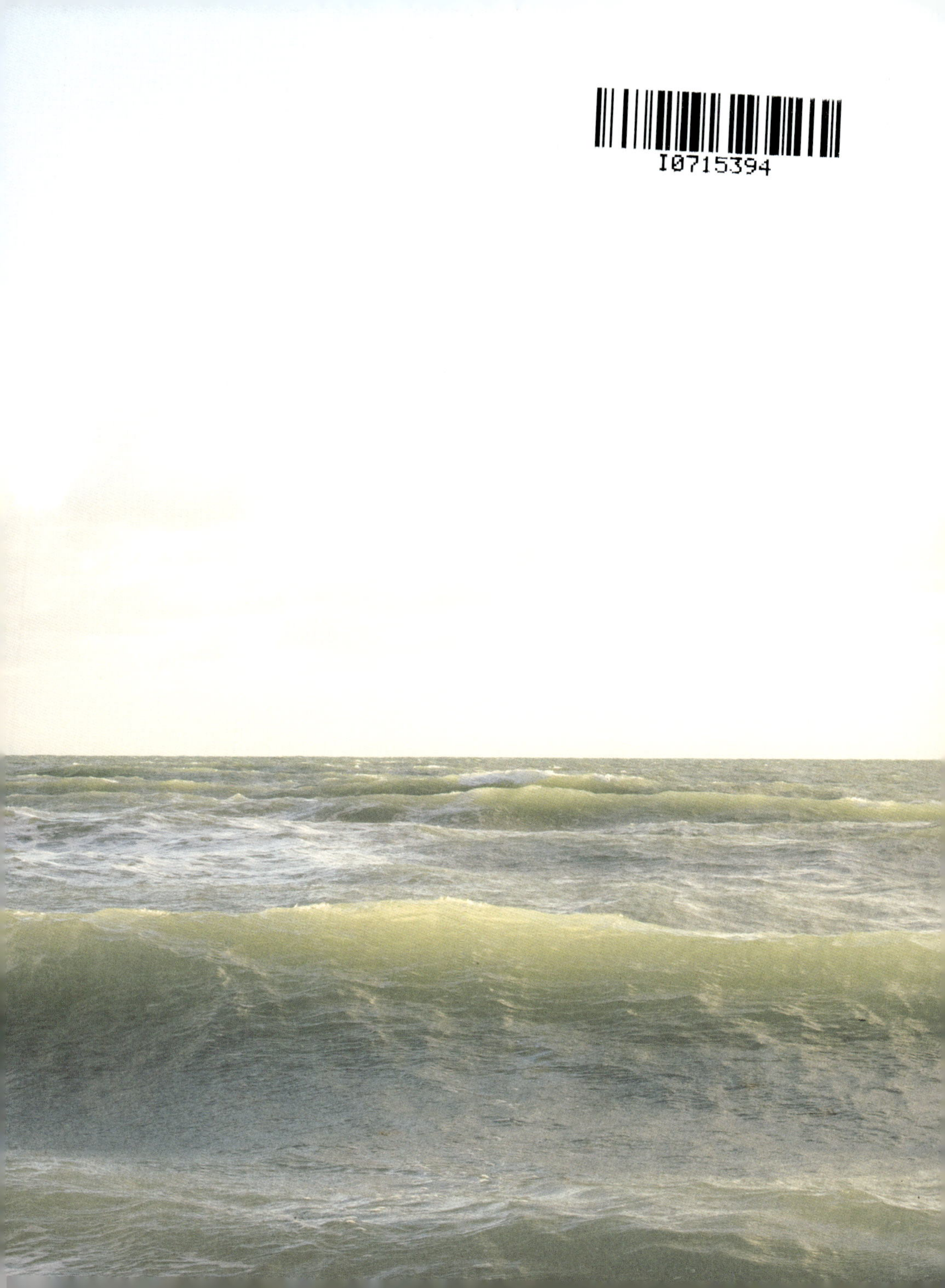

I0715394

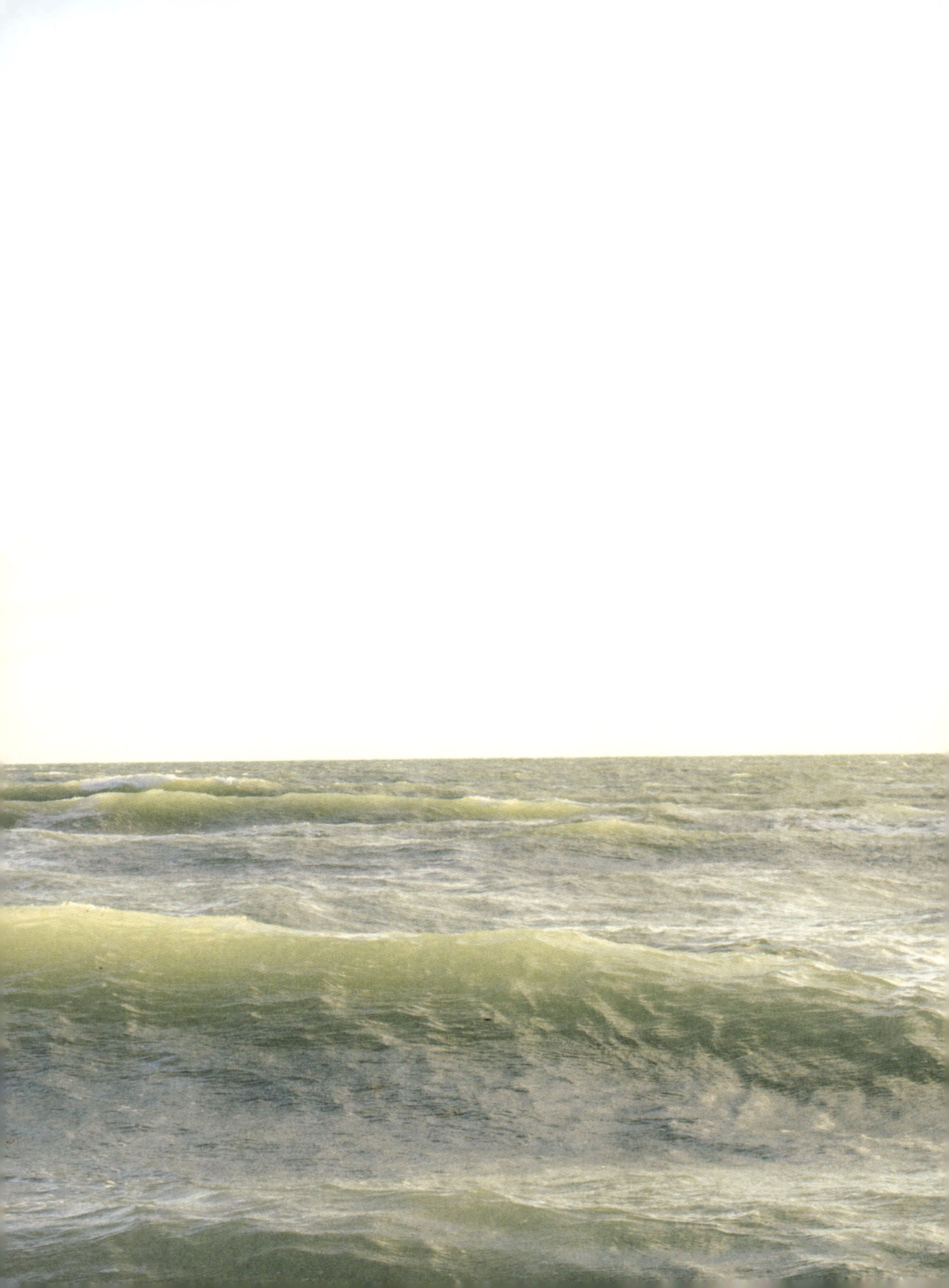

Lifeguard Towers: Miami

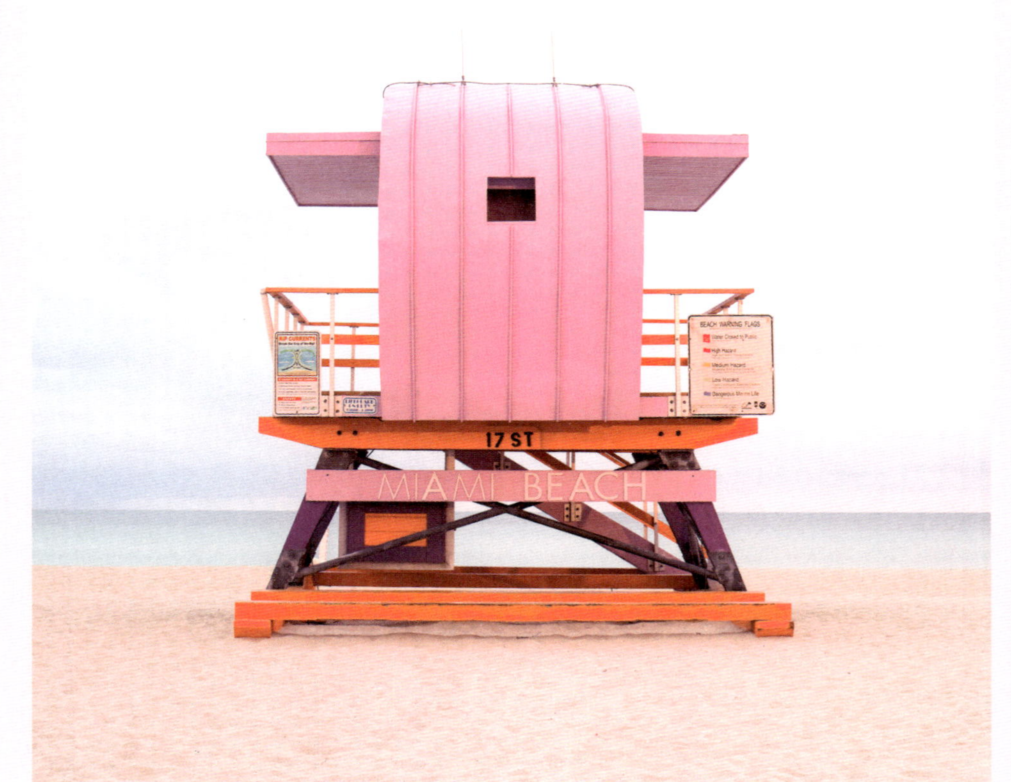

BEACH WARNING FLAGS
Water Closed to Public
High Hazard
Medium Hazard
Low Hazard
Dangerous Marine Life
17 ST
MIAMI BEACH

# Lifeguard Towers: Miami

## Tommy Kwak

Introduction by Karen Taylor Quinn

Blurring Books | Brooklyn, NY

Miami

85th St.
81st St.
80th St.
77th St.
74th St.
72nd St.
69th St.
67th St.
64th St.
60th St.
57th St.
55th St.
53rd St.
50th St.
46th St.
43rd St.
41st St.
35th St.
30th St.
26th St.
24th St.
21st St.
18th St
17th St.
Lincoln Rd.
15th St.
14th St.
13th St.
12th St.
10th St.
8th St.
6th St.
5th St.
4th St.
3rd St.
1st St.
100
Jetty
Miami
Beach
1 mile

# INTRODUCTION

I first encountered Tommy Kwak's photography in a gallery window in Brooklyn. The images—flocks of seagulls against a pale sky—were uniquely transportive: I could almost taste the ocean spray. This vivid sense of place, expressed in Kwak's images through graphic, minimalist composition and kaleidoscopic color, characterizes much of his art.

Kwak's *Lifeguard Towers* series, which depicts seaside structures in California, New York, and Miami, is no exception. Painted in candy-coated hues of pink and purple, yellow and green, the Miami towers embody a splashy mid-90s style that's now back in vogue. They were commissioned by the city of Miami in 1995 as part of a rebuild effort after Hurricane Andrew, with new towers added in 2015, dotting the eight-mile stretch of shoreline with color and style. Kwak first encountered them four years later, in 2019. Immediately "I was hooked," he said. The pink tower on 17th Street was the first one he photographed, and thus began a years-long obsession.

In Kwak's images, the towers become characters, each with its own personality and flair. The repeated, straight-on composition highlights each structure's idiosyncrasies, and the sea and sky behind them act as a mood meter. "My ideal condition was an overcast and drizzly day," Kwak wrote, "so the backdrop of sea and sky were as minimal as possible for the towers to stand out." Therein lies a creative tension that Kwak draws on often: on one hand, he strives for objective documentation, to present subjects "as purely as possible." And yet, the precise and consistent proportions—and his attraction to bright, saturated color—lend the images a whimsical and almost surreal beauty. They are at once familiar and otherworldly.

I asked Kwak what draws him to the sea. Though he didn't spend much time at the beach as a child, he has always found a peculiar freedom by the water: "it brings a sense of openness and clarity," he told me. "And aesthetically I'm drawn to the simplicity of horizon, sky, and sea—minimal and endless at the same time."

Karen Taylor Quinn
*Director of Social Media at The New Yorker*

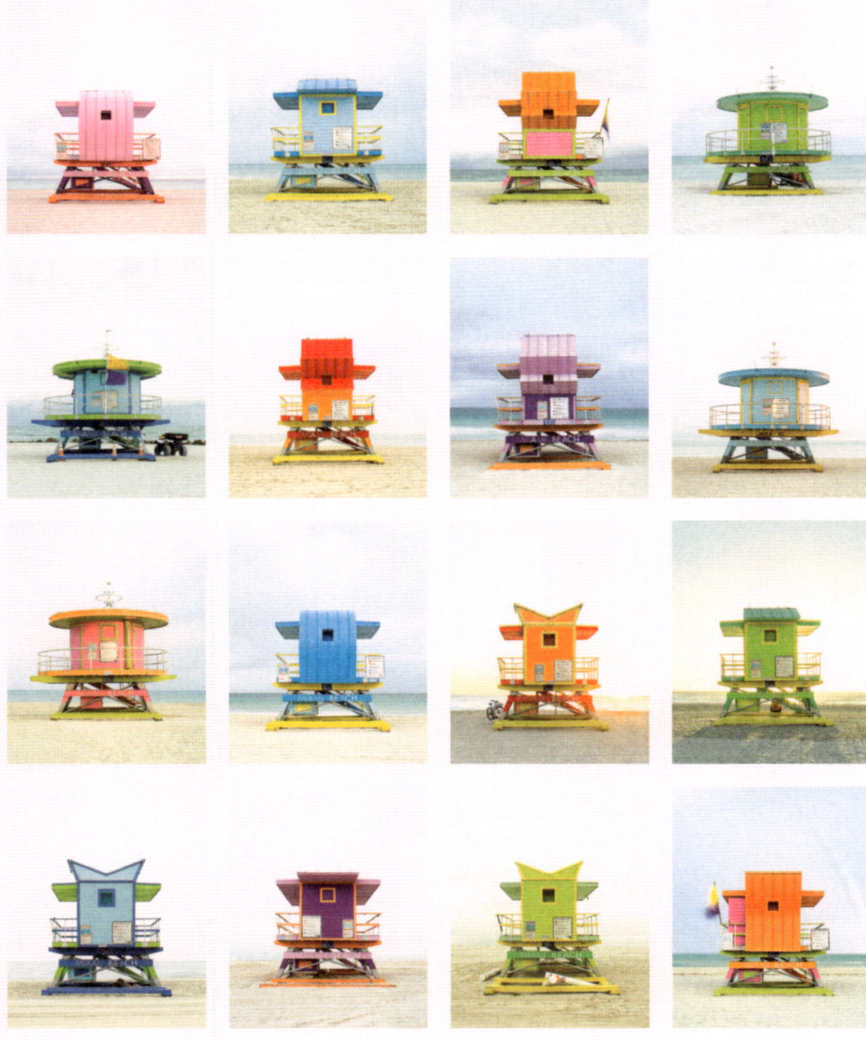

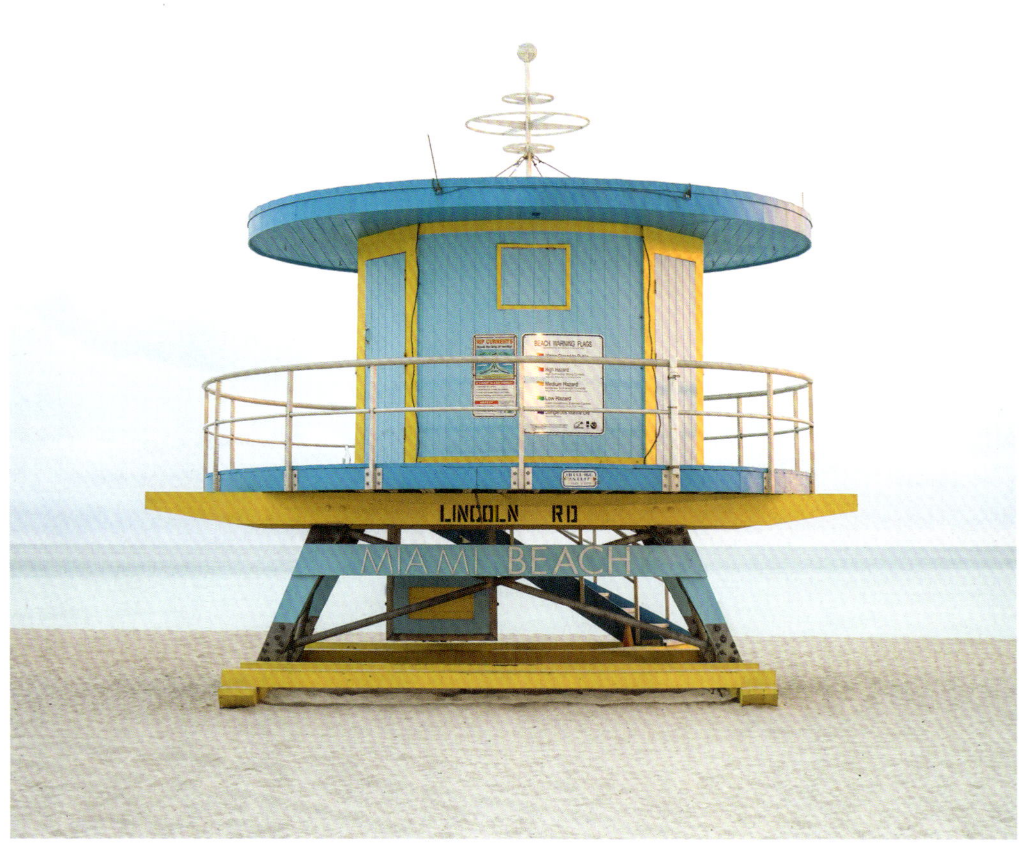

LINCOLN RD
MIAMI BEACH

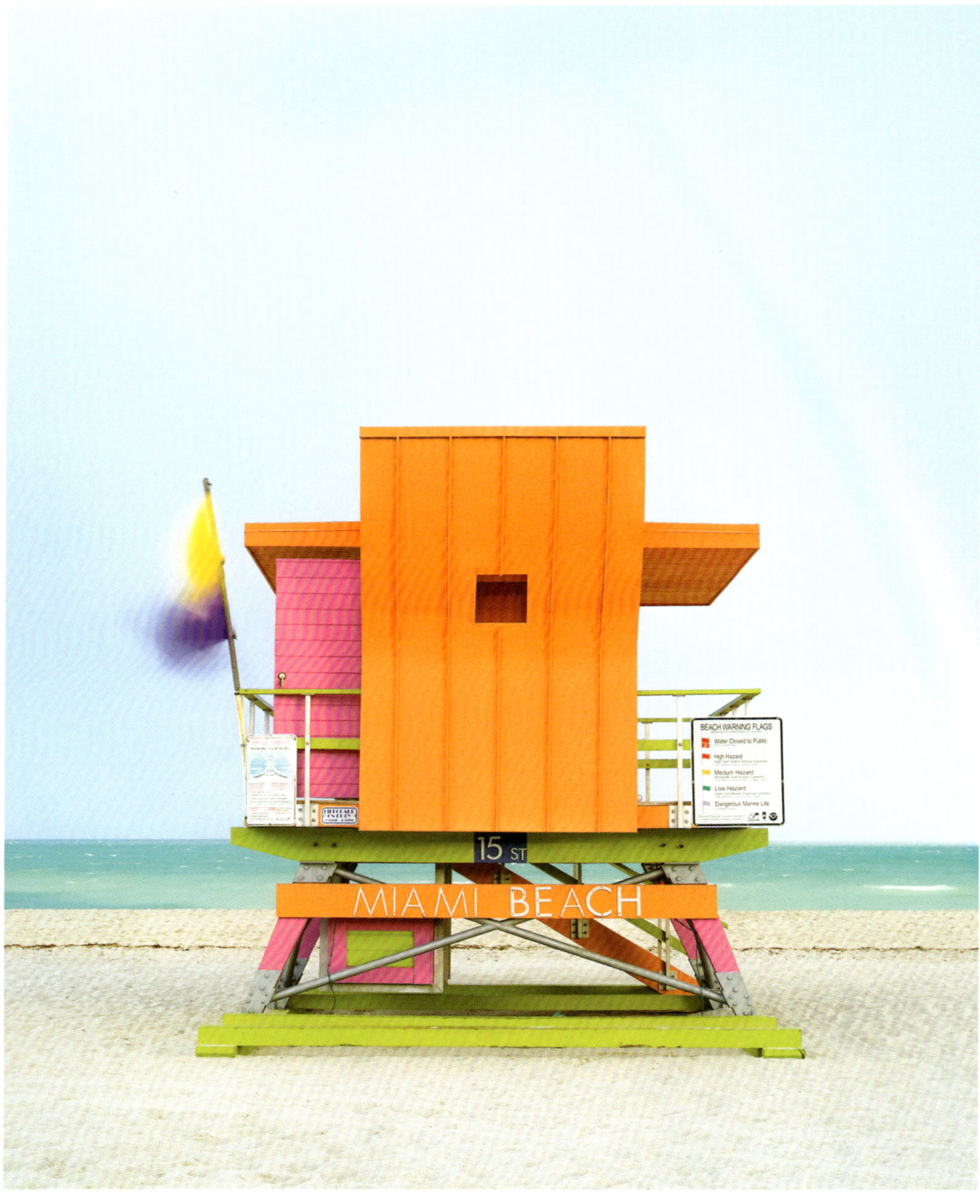
BEACH WARNING FLAGS
Water Closed to Public
High Hazard
Medium Hazard
Low Hazard
Dangerous Marine Life
15 ST
MIAMI BEACH

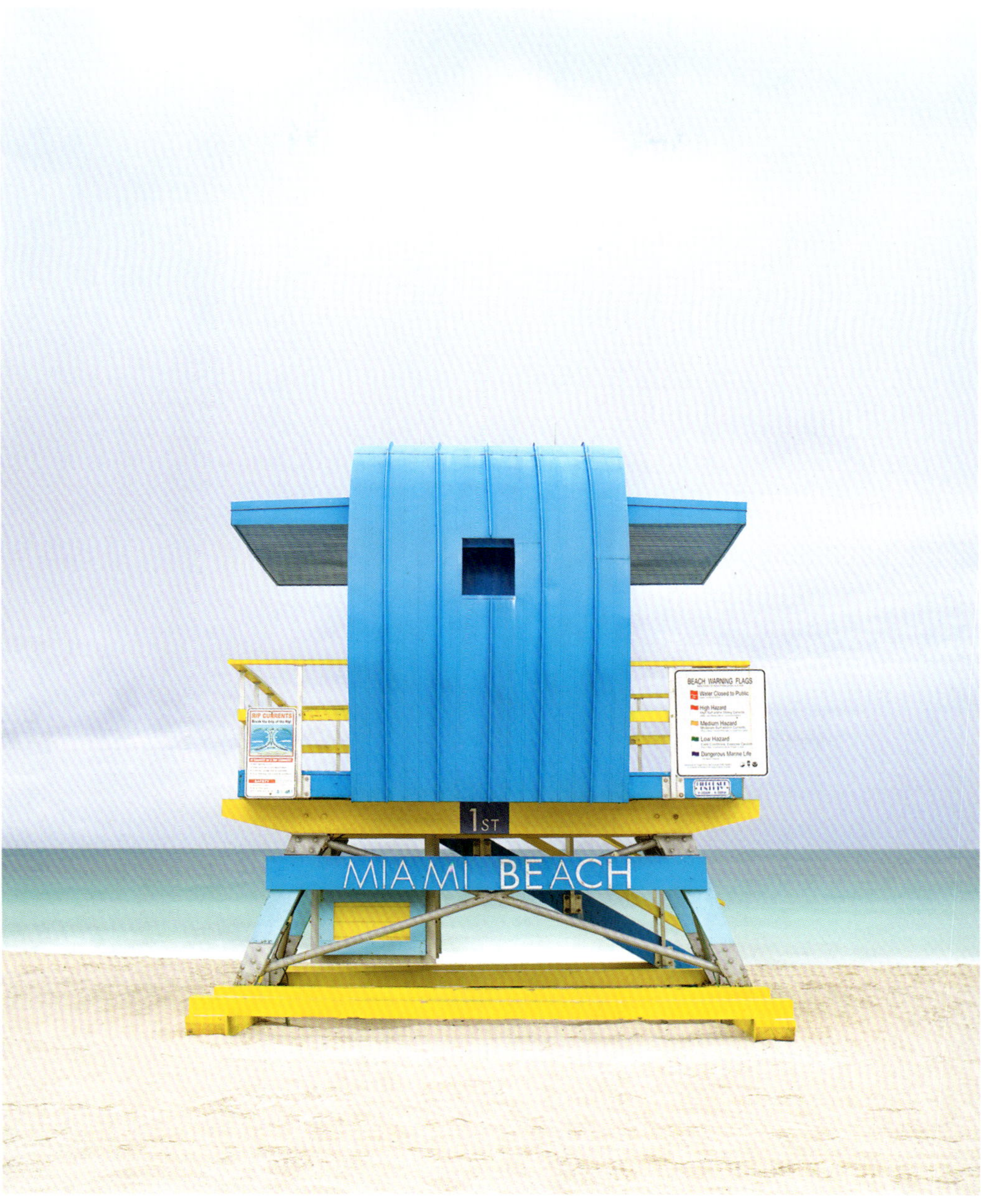
BEACH WARNING FLAGS
Water Closed to Public
High Hazard
Medium Hazard
Low Hazard
Dangerous Marine Life
RIP CURRENTS
1ST
MIAMI BEACH

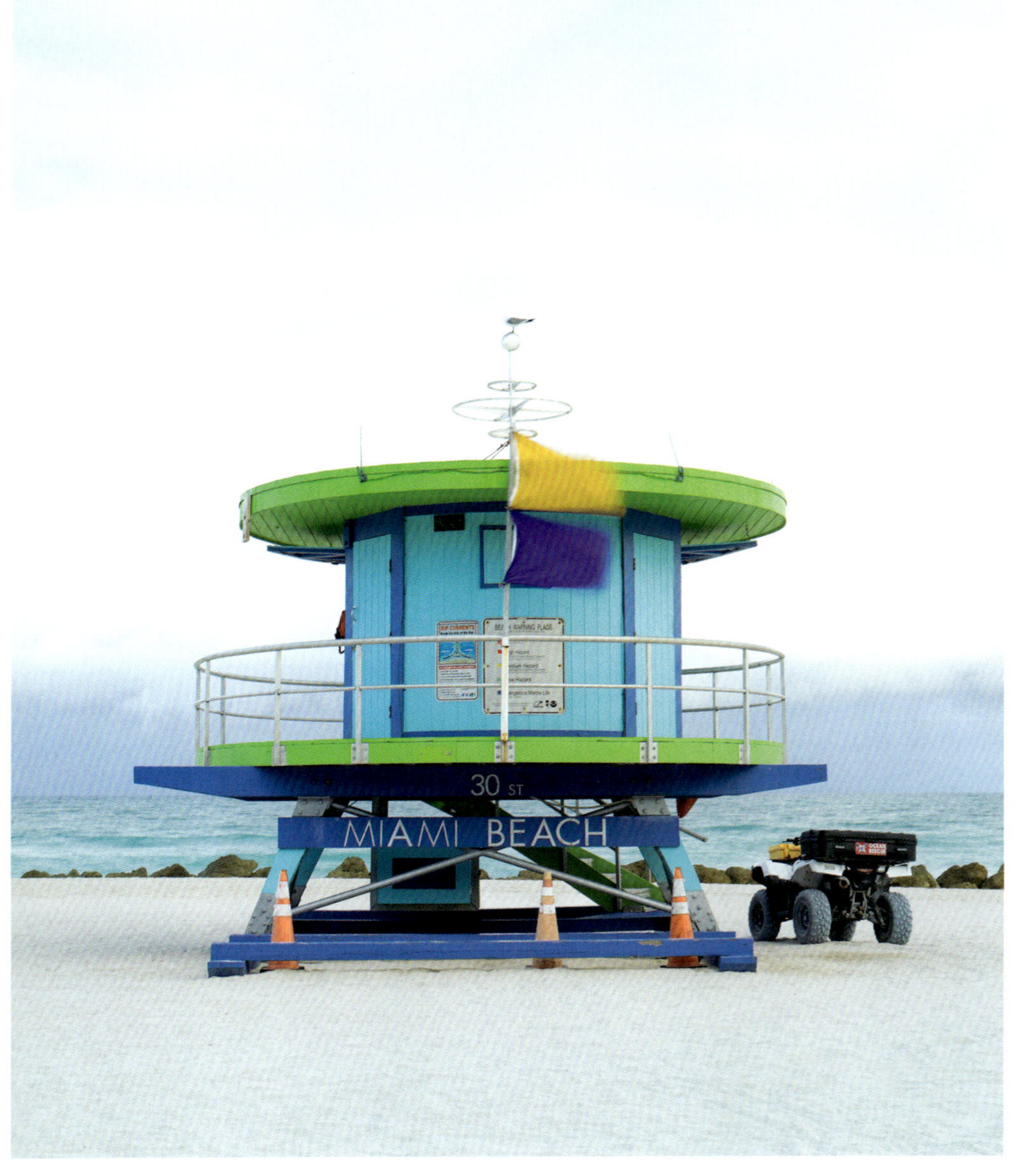

30 ST
MIAMI BEACH
OCEAN RESCUE

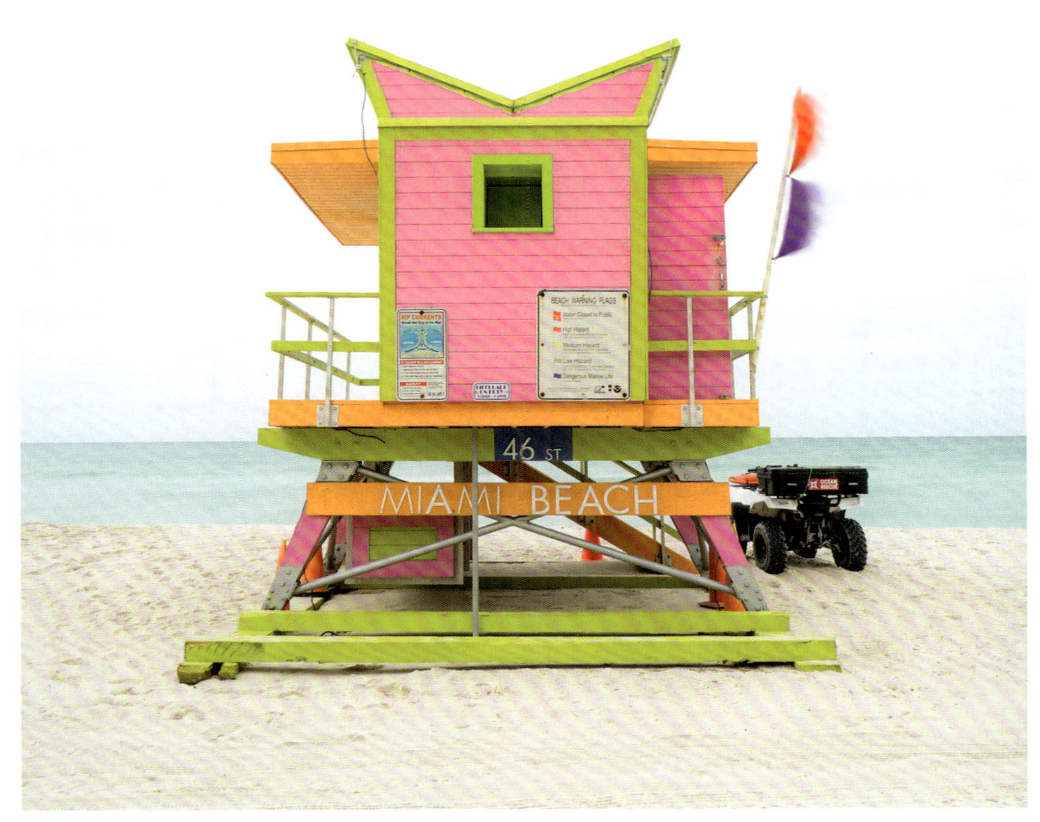
46 ST
MIAMI BEACH
BEACH WARNING FLAGS
RIP CURRENTS
OCEAN RESCUE

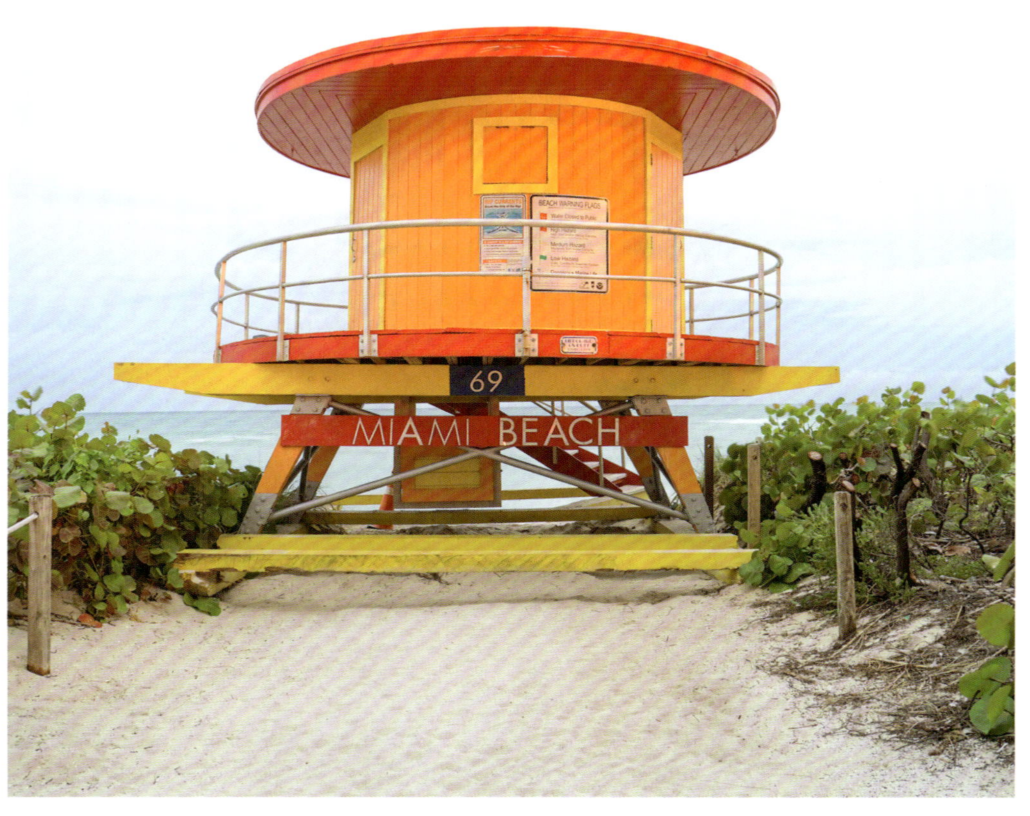
BEACH WARNING FLAGS
69
MIAMI BEACH

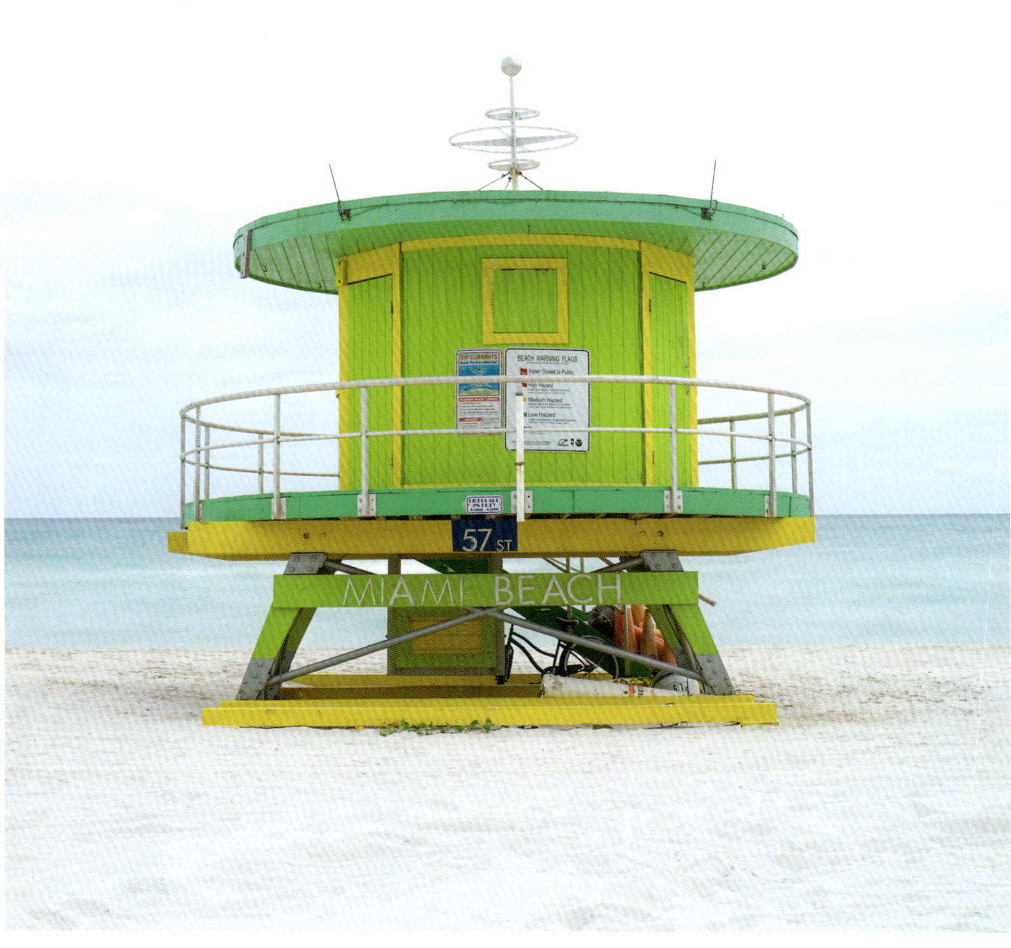

RIP CURRENTS
BEACH WARNING FLAGS
Water Closed to Public
High Hazard
Medium Hazard
Low Hazard
57 ST
MIAMI BEACH

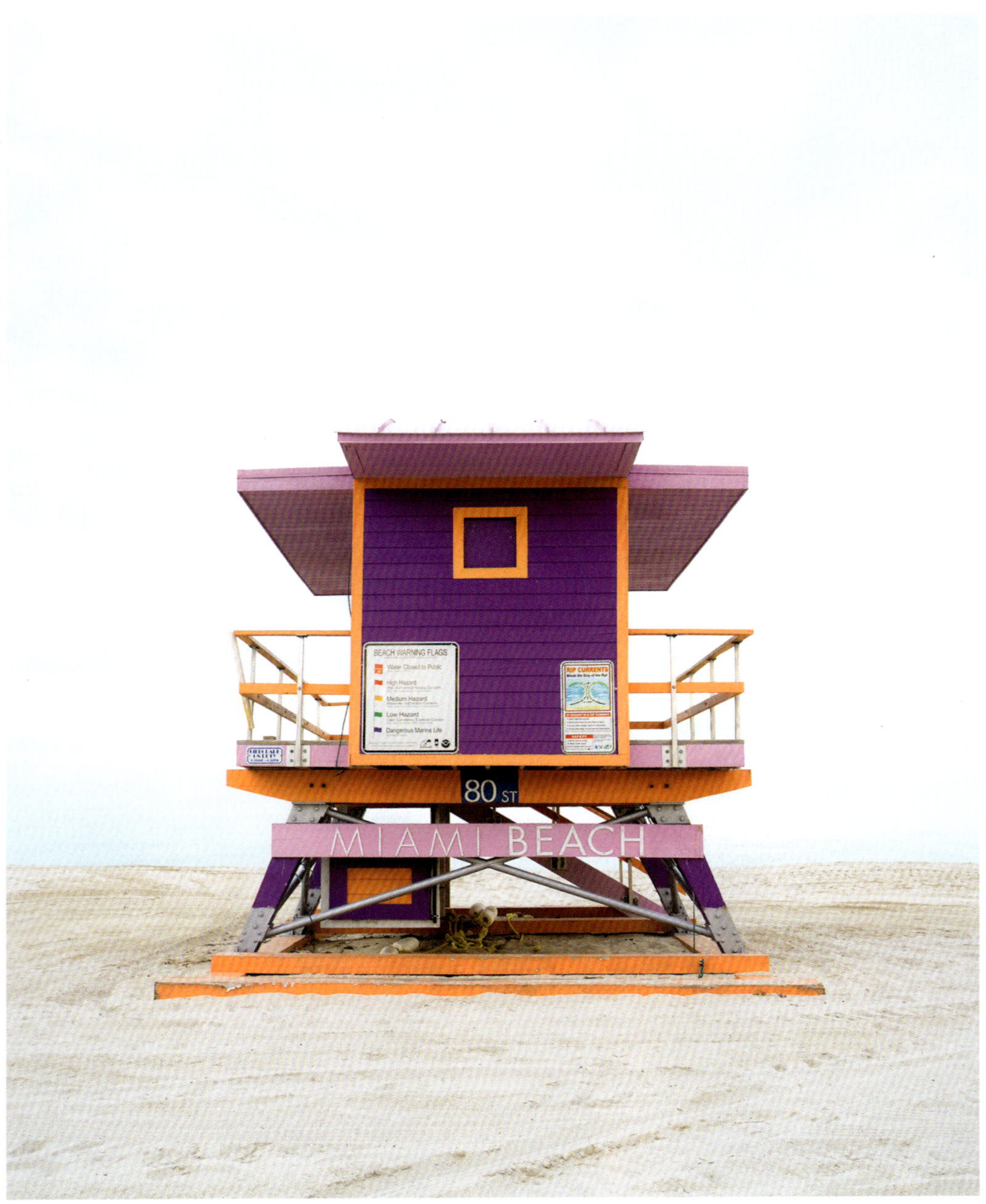
BEACH WARNING FLAGS
Water Closed to Public
High Hazard
Medium Hazard
Low Hazard
Dangerous Marine Life
RIP CURRENTS
80 ST
MIAMI BEACH

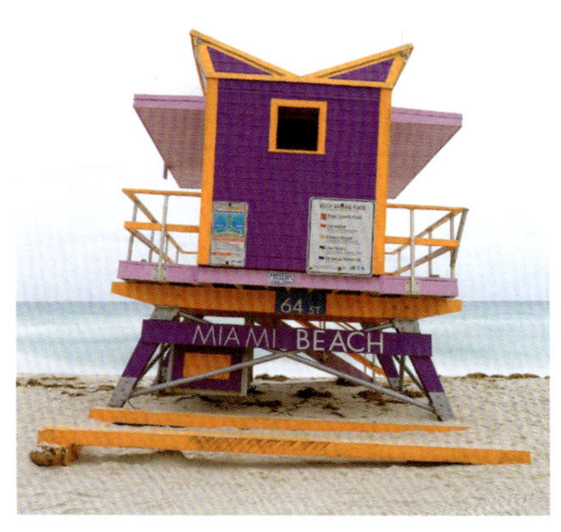
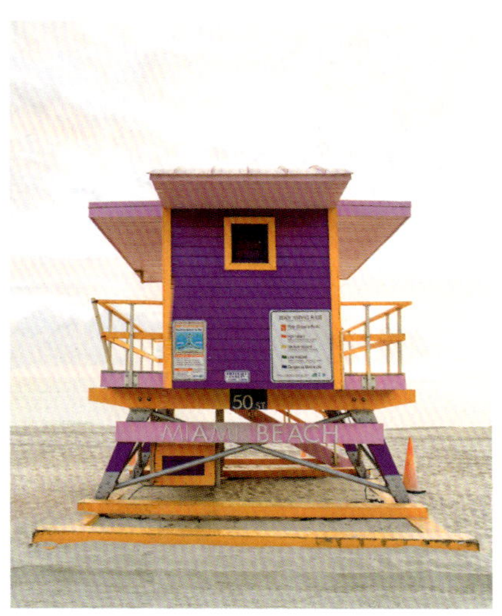

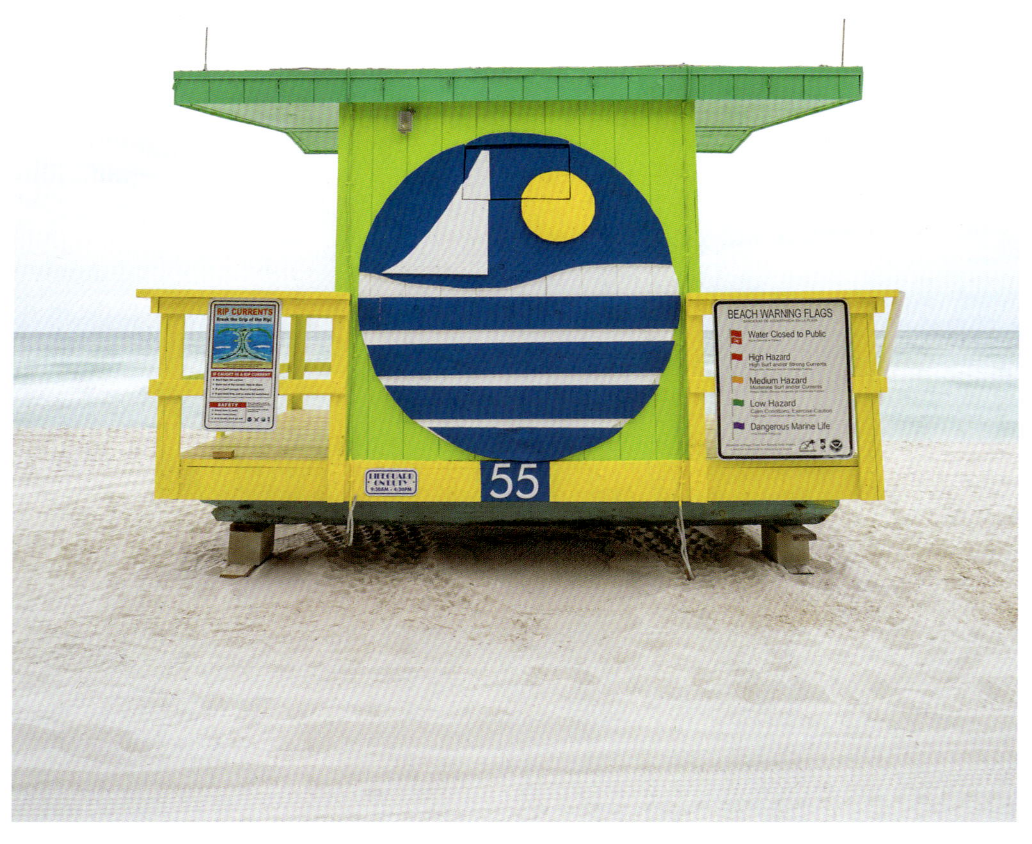
RIP CURRENTS
Break the Grip of the Rip!
BEACH WARNING FLAGS
Water Closed to Public
High Hazard
High Surf and/or Strong Currents
Medium Hazard
Moderate Surf and/or Currents
Low Hazard
Calm Conditions, Exercise Caution
Dangerous Marine Life
55

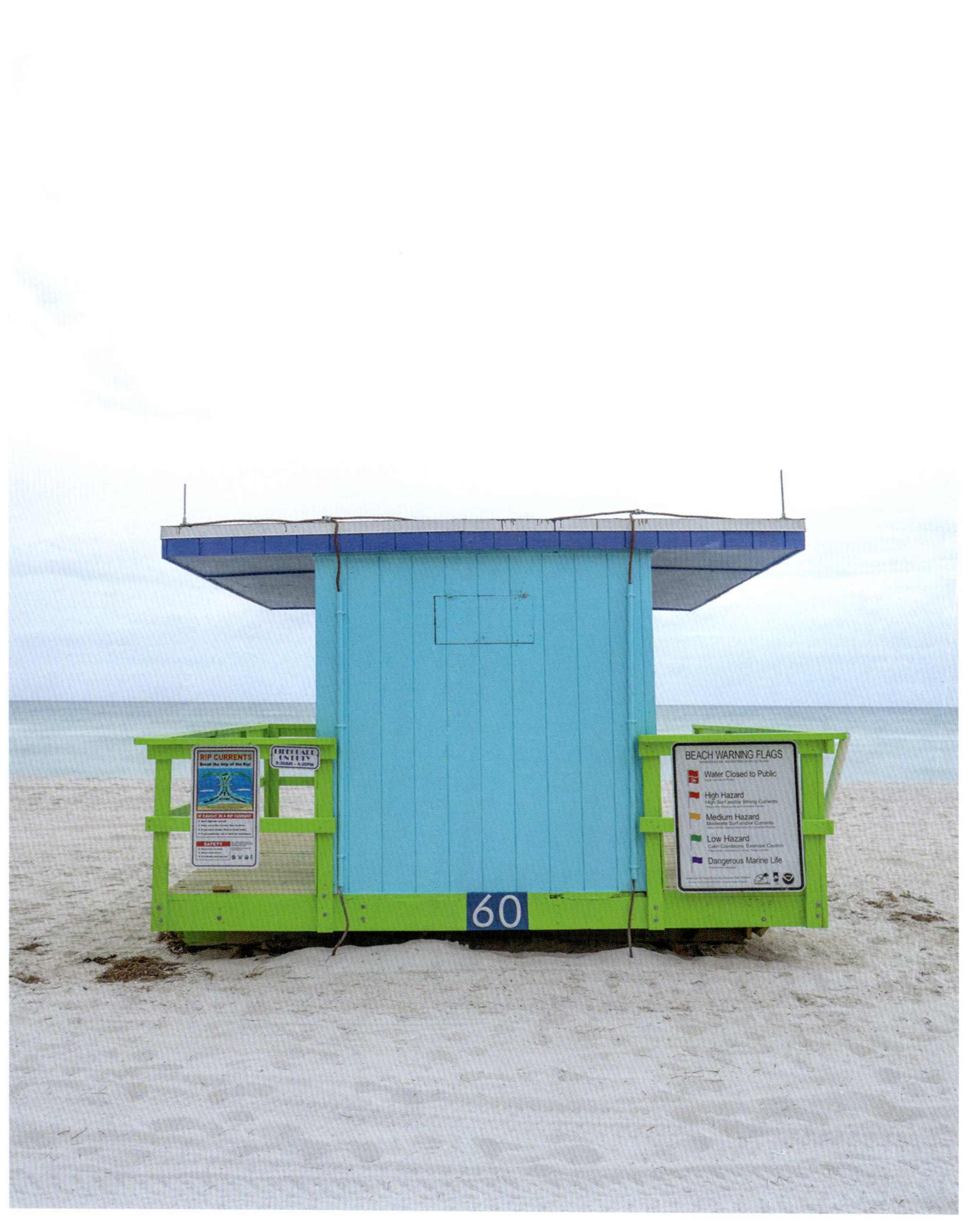
RIP CURRENTS
Break the Grip of the Rip!
IF CAUGHT IN A RIP CURRENT
SAFETY
BEACH WARNING FLAGS
Water Closed to Public
High Hazard
High Surf and/or Strong Currents
Medium Hazard
Moderate Surf and/or Currents
Low Hazard
Calm Conditions, Exercise Caution
Dangerous Marine Life
60

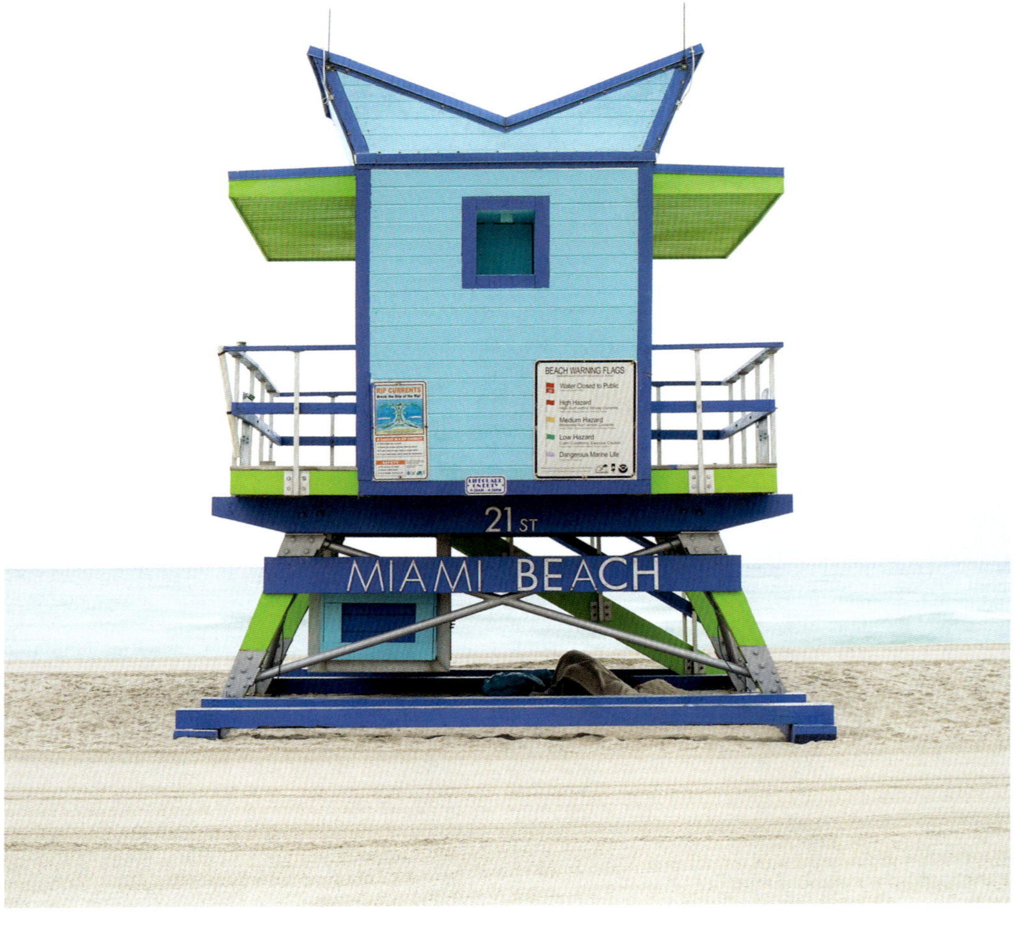
RIP CURRENTS
Break the Grip of the Rip!

BEACH WARNING FLAGS
Water Closed to Public
High Hazard
Medium Hazard
Low Hazard
Dangerous Marine Life

21ST
MIAMI BEACH

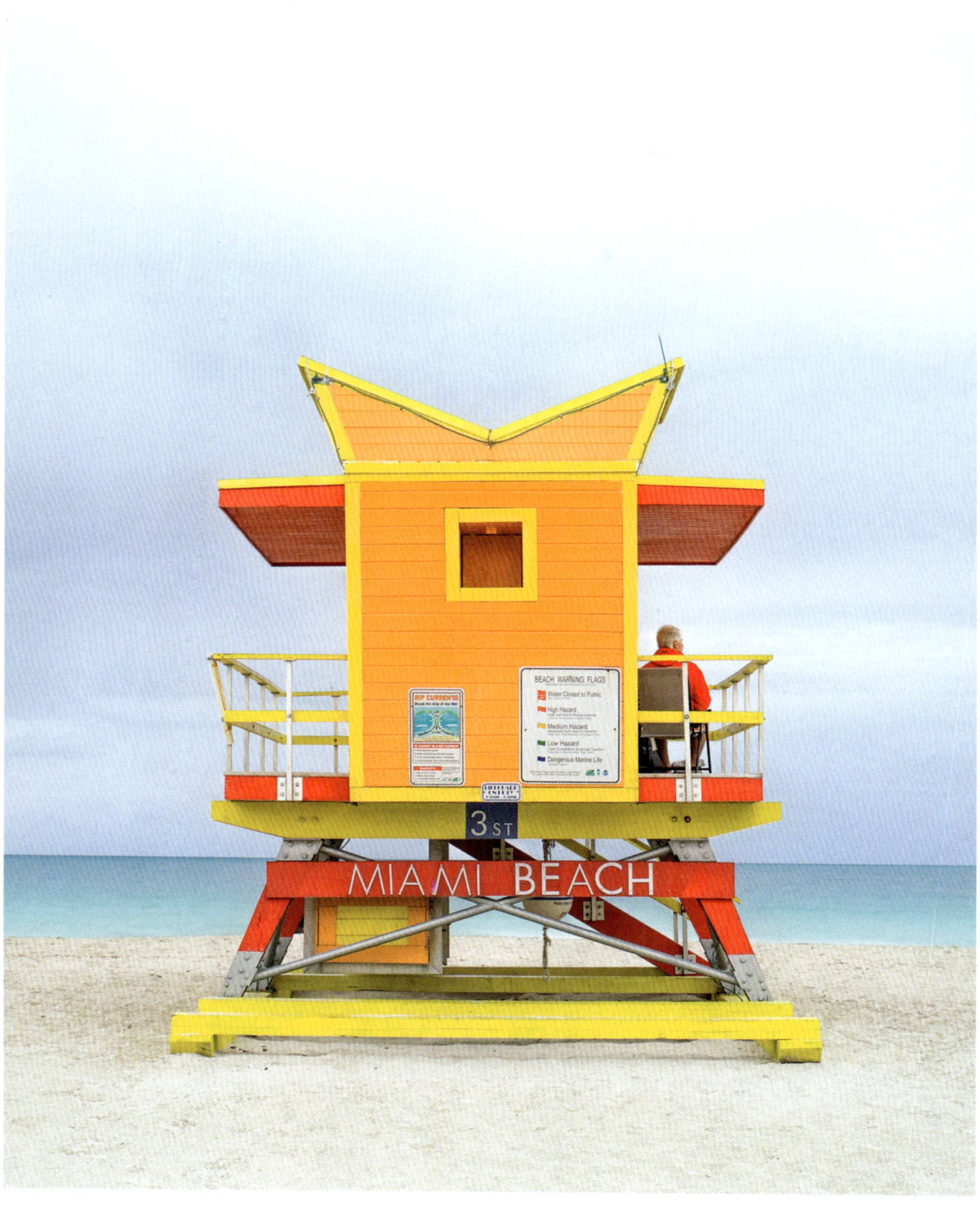

BEACH WARNING FLAGS
Water Closed to Public
High Hazard
Medium Hazard
Low Hazard
Dangerous Marine Life
3 ST
MIAMI BEACH

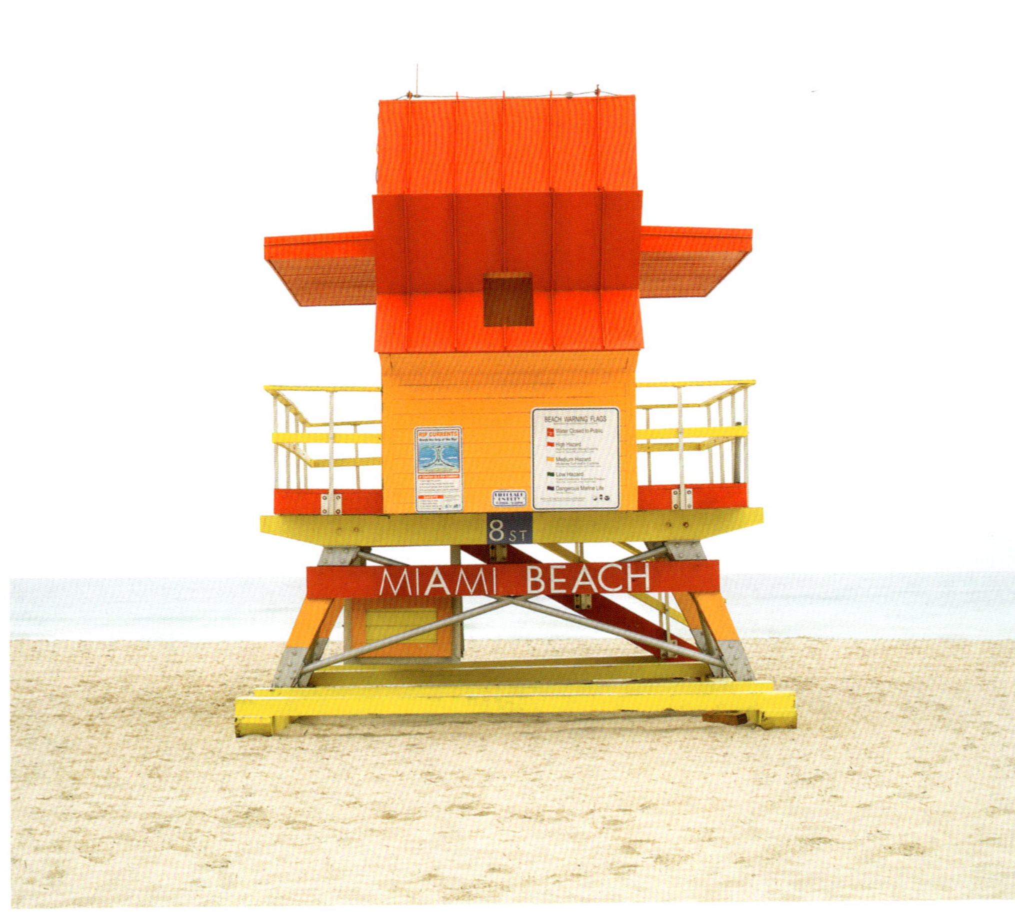
8 ST
MIAMI BEACH
BEACH WARNING FLAGS
RIP CURRENTS

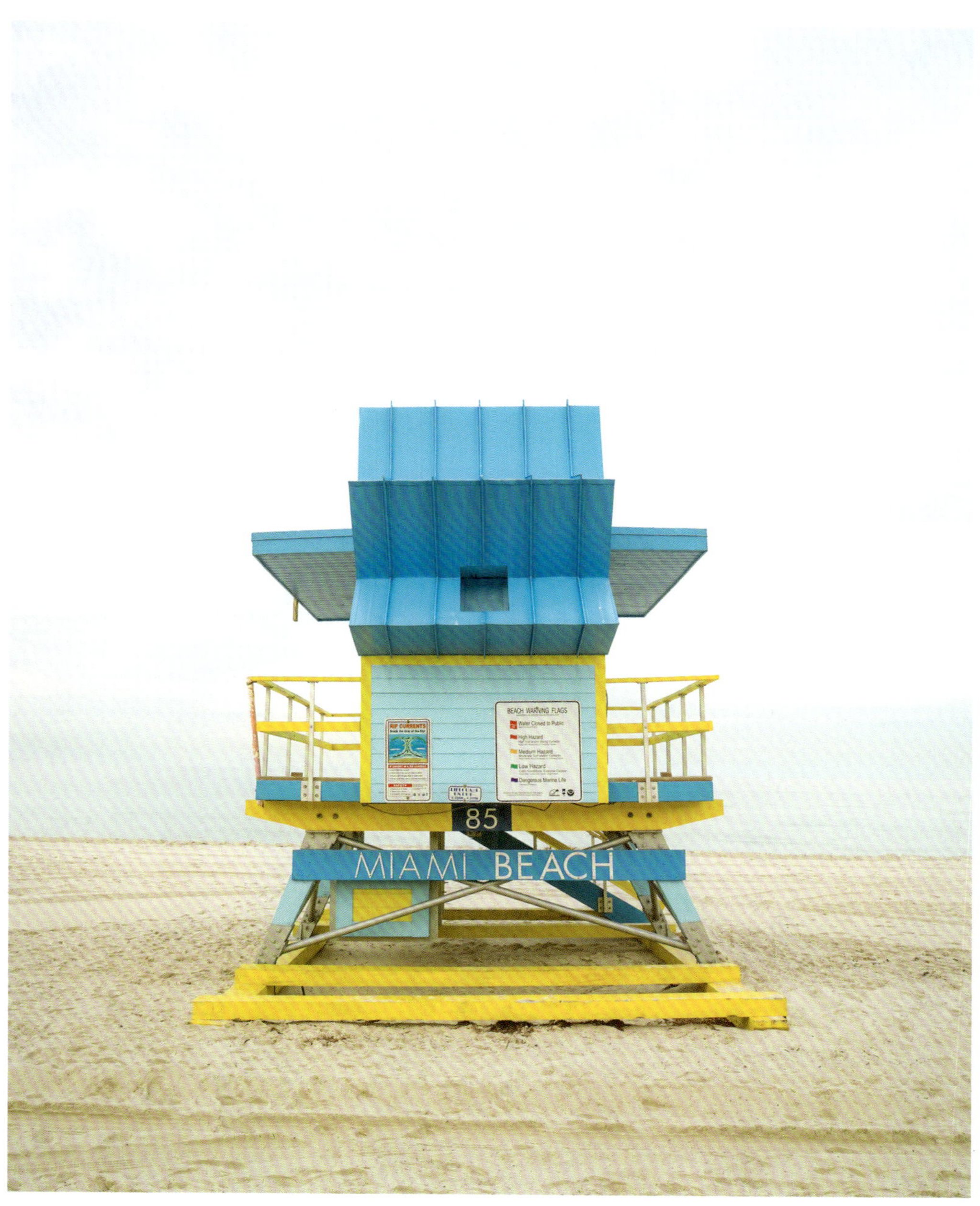
MIAMI BEACH
85

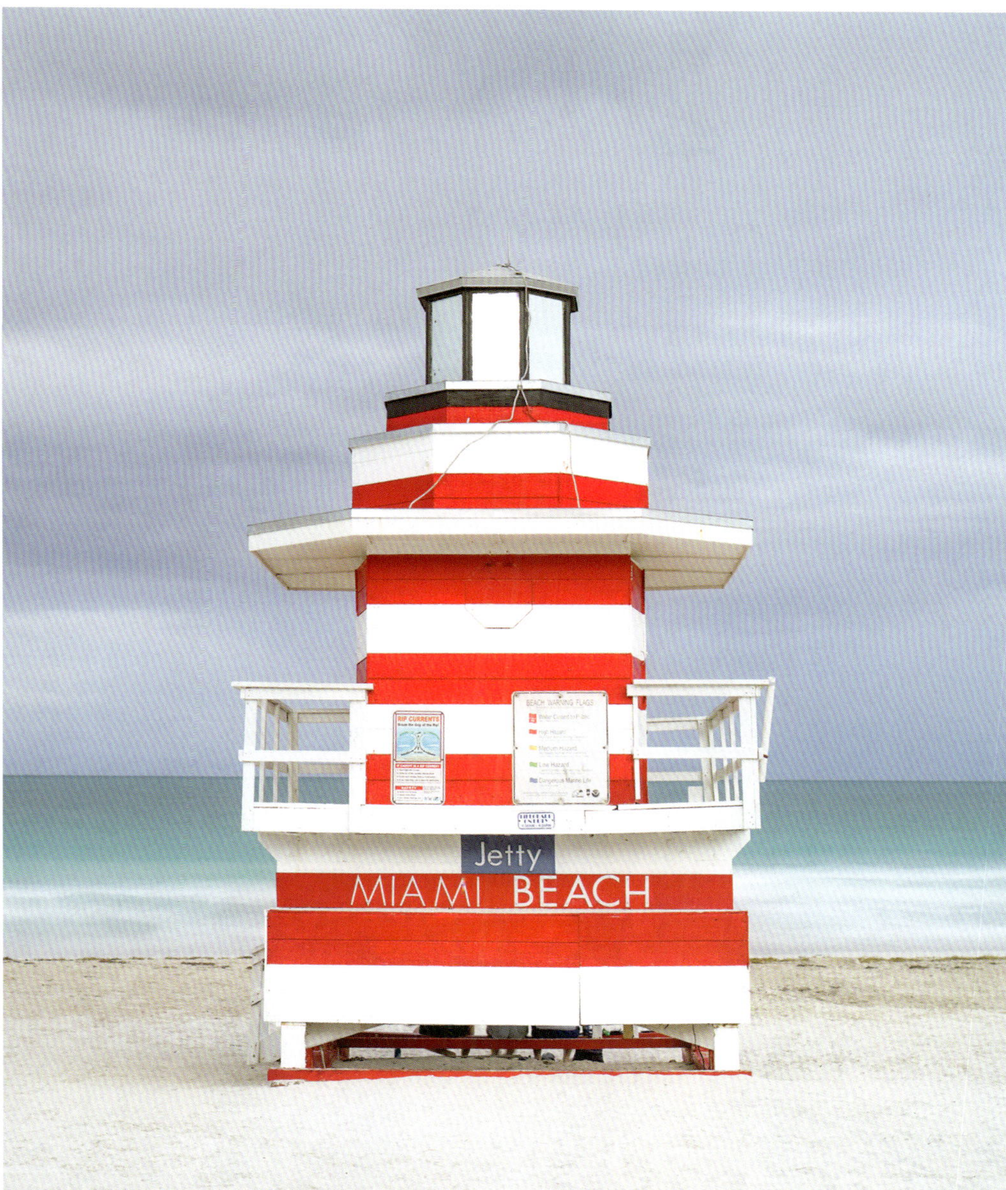
Jetty
MIAMI BEACH
RIP CURRENTS
BEACH WARNING FLAGS

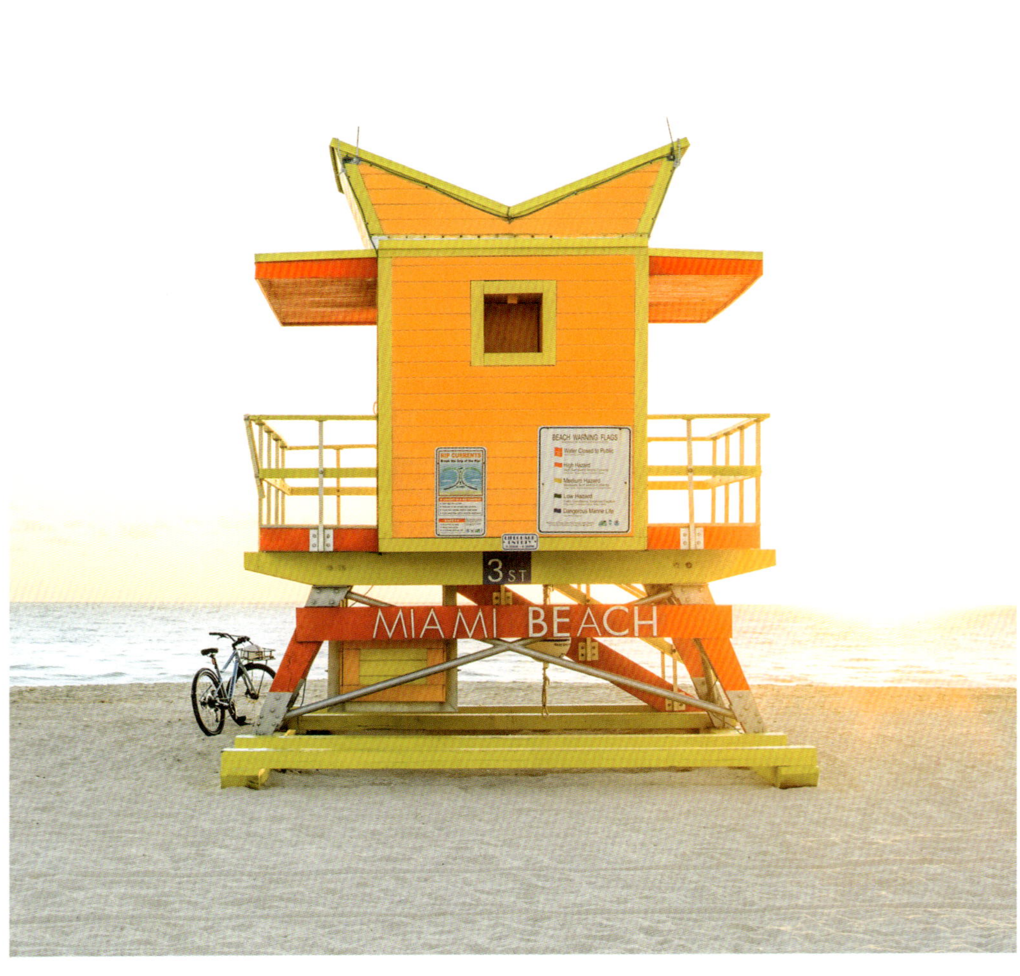
MIAMI BEACH
3 ST
BEACH WARNING FLAGS
RIP CURRENTS

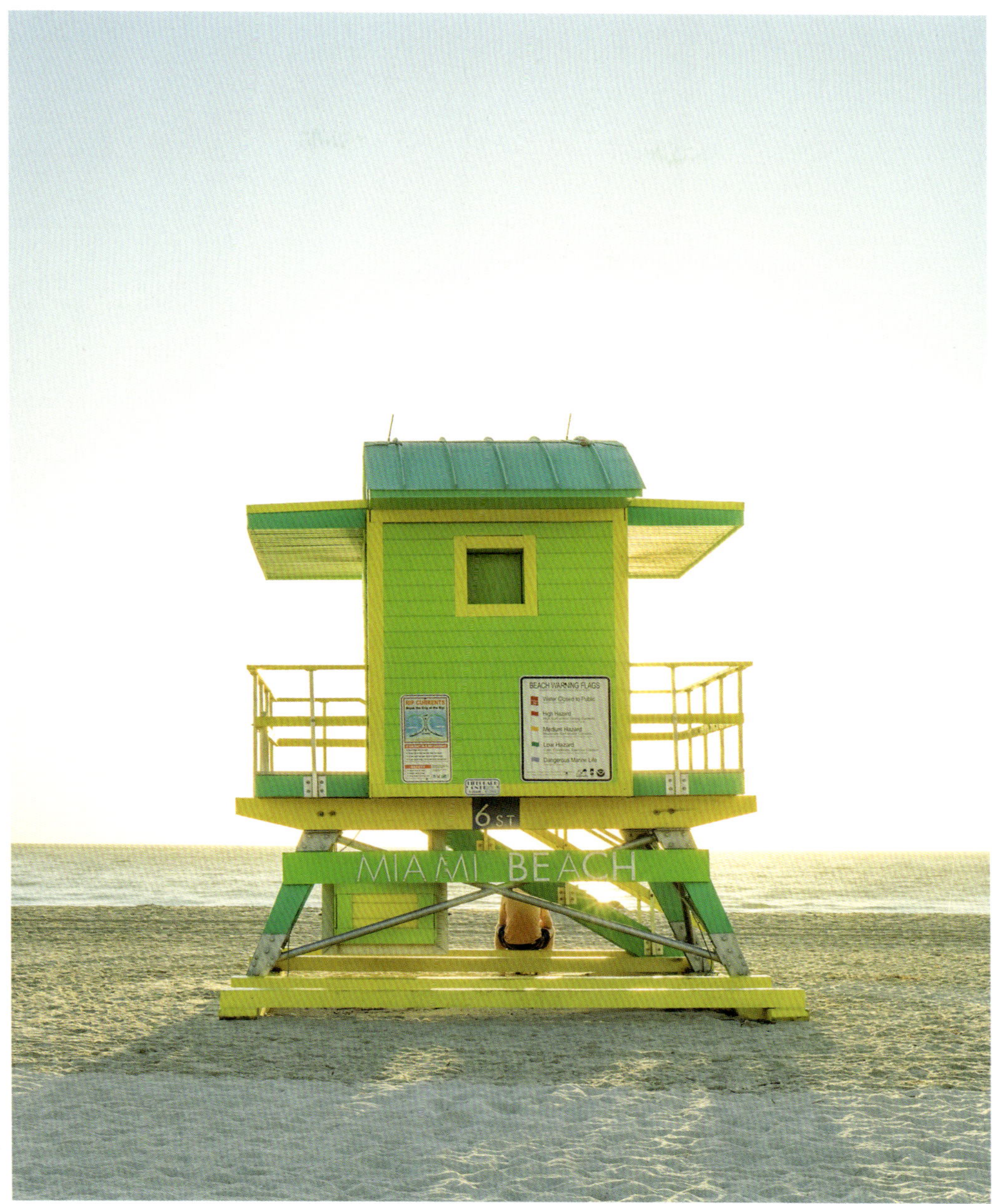
BEACH WARNING FLAGS
Water Closed to Public
High Hazard
Medium Hazard
Low Hazard
Dangerous Marine Life
6 ST
MIAMI BEACH

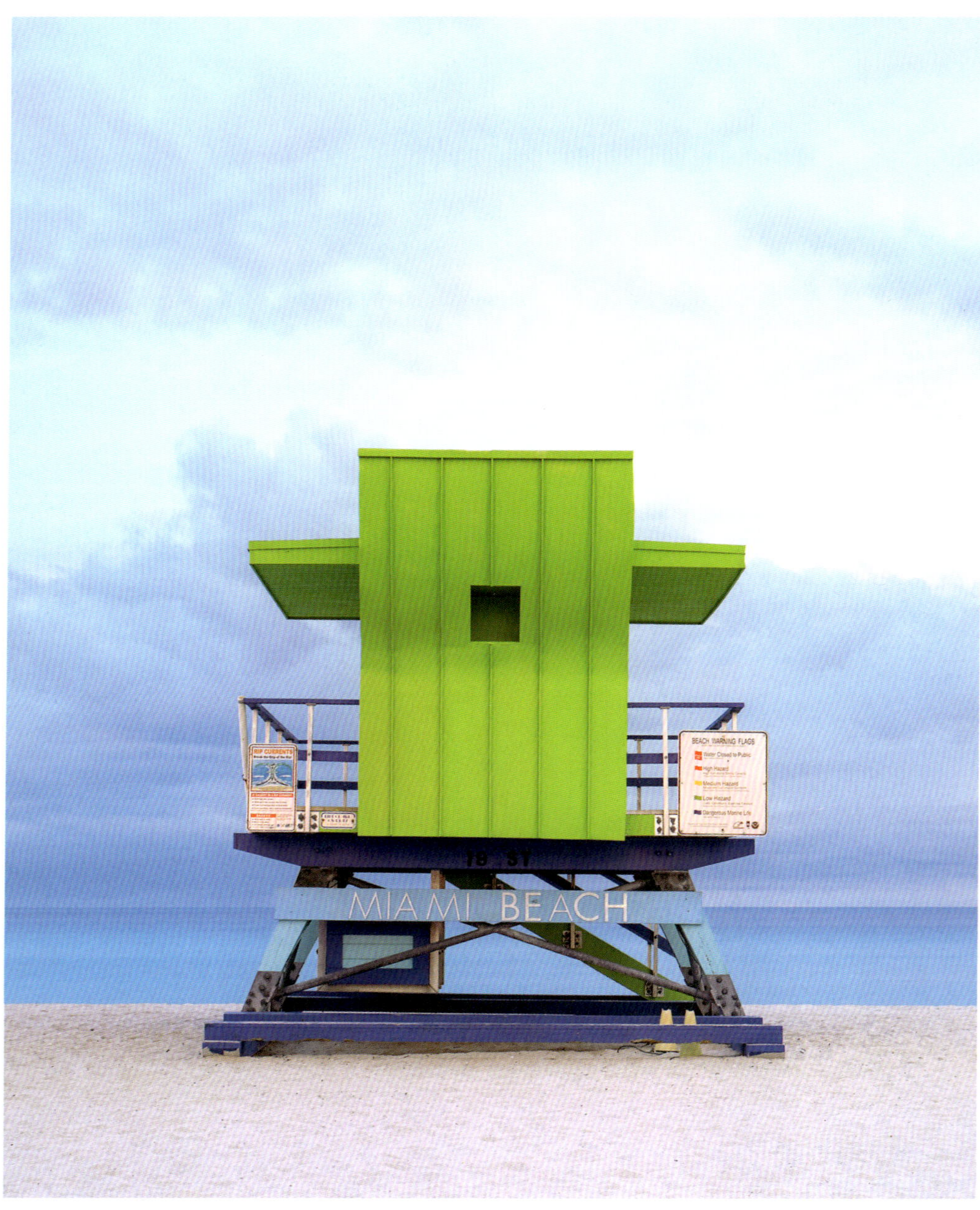
MIAMI BEACH

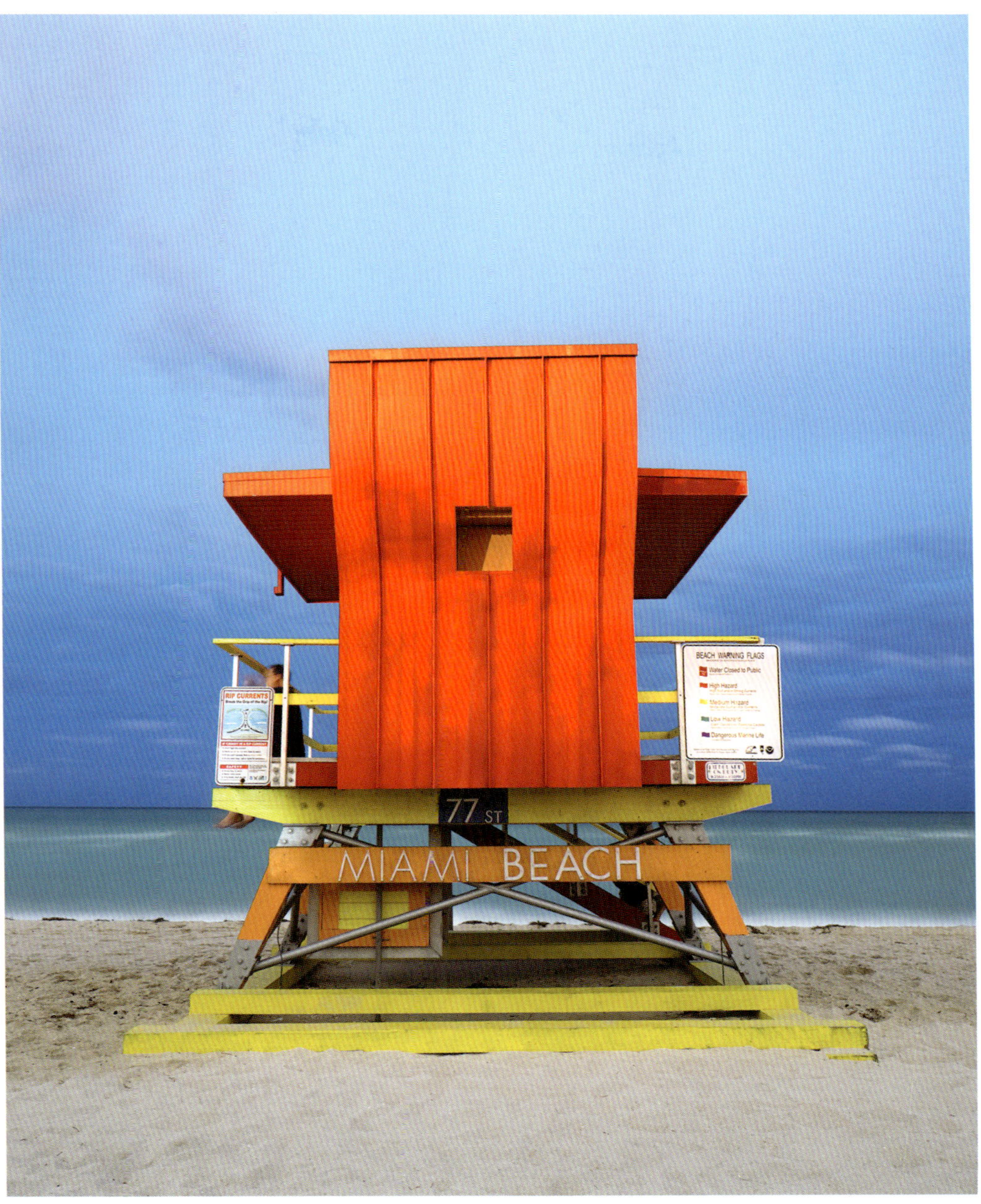
BEACH WARNING FLAGS
Water Closed to Public
High Hazard
Medium Hazard
Low Hazard
Dangerous Marine Life
RIP CURRENTS
Break the Grip of the Rip!
IF CAUGHT IN A RIP CURRENT
SAFETY
77 ST
MIAMI BEACH

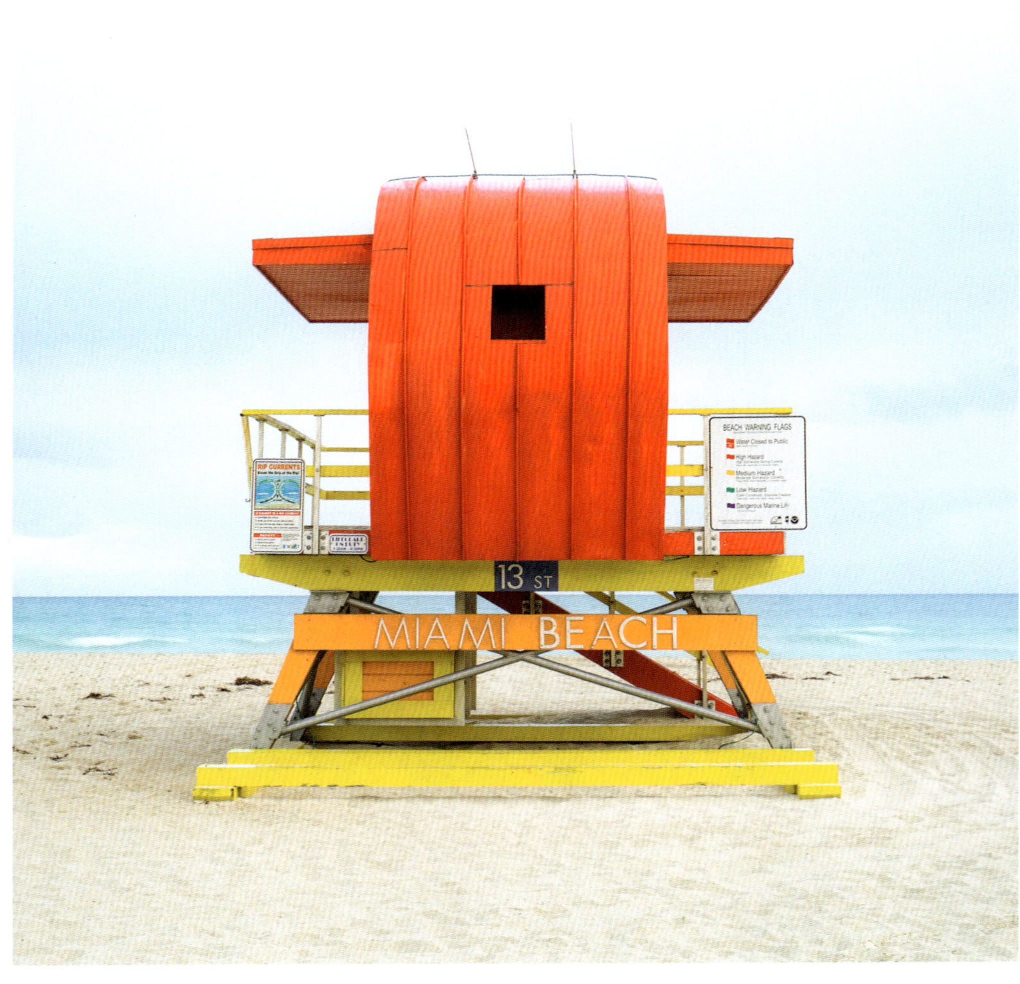

BEACH WARNING FLAGS
RIP CURRENTS
13 ST
MIAMI BEACH

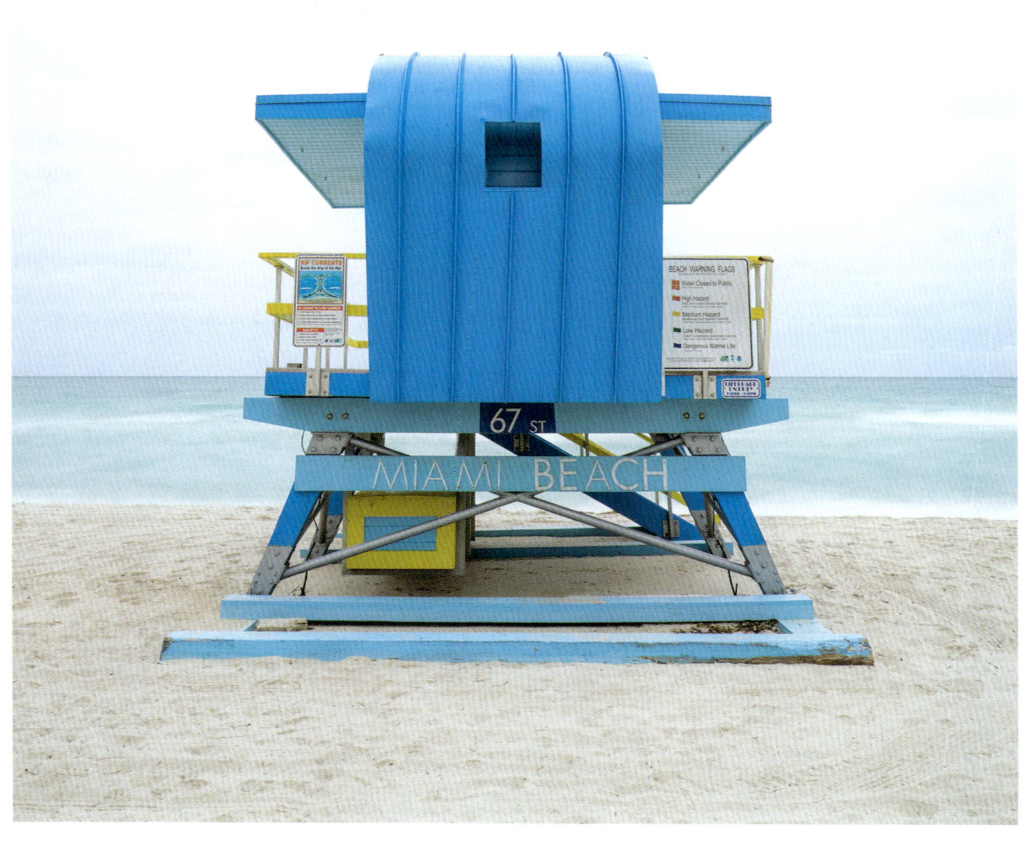
67 ST
MIAMI BEACH
RIP CURRENTS
BEACH WARNING FLAGS
Water Closed to Public
High Hazard
Medium Hazard
Low Hazard
Dangerous Marine Life

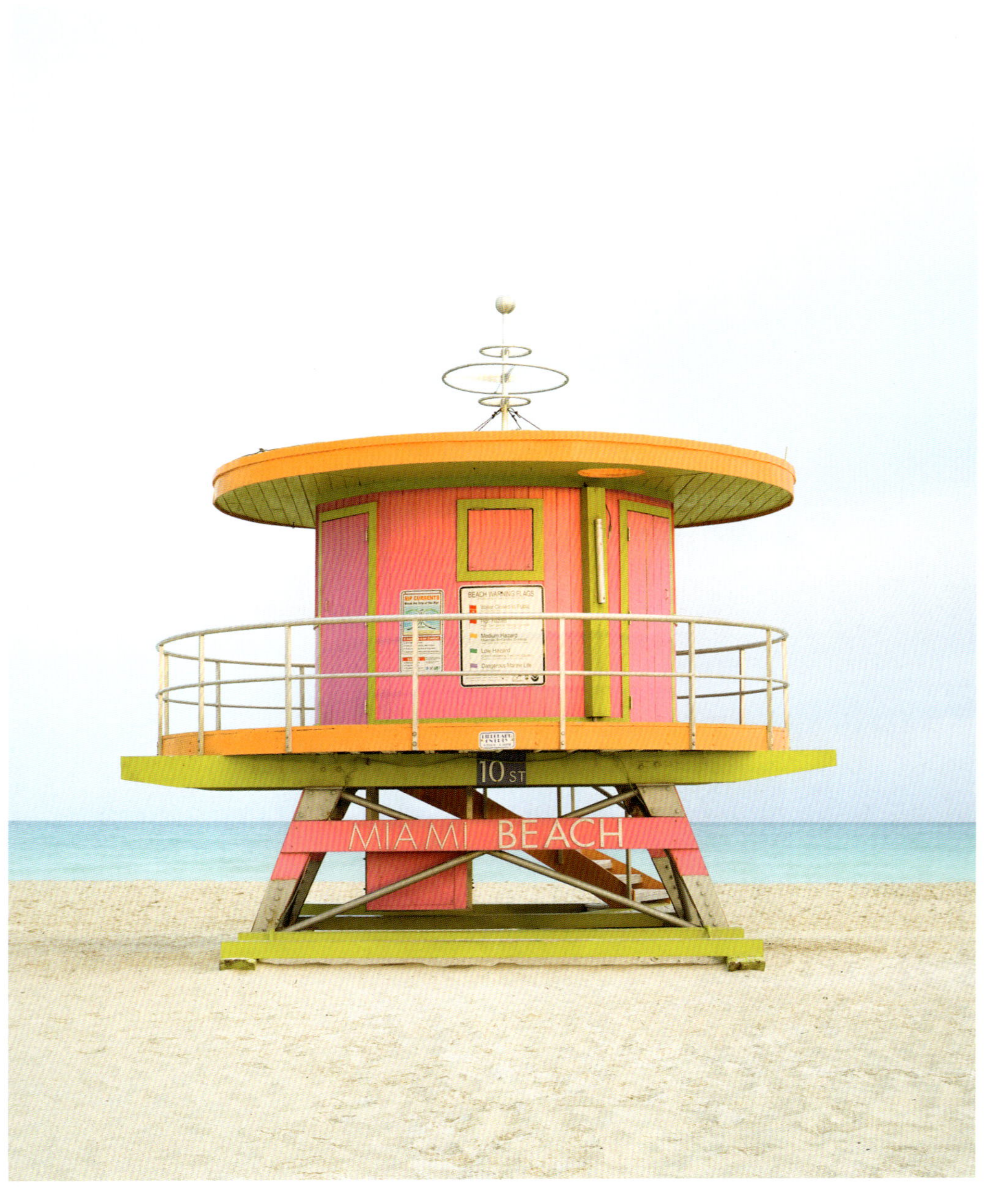

MIAMI BEACH
10 ST

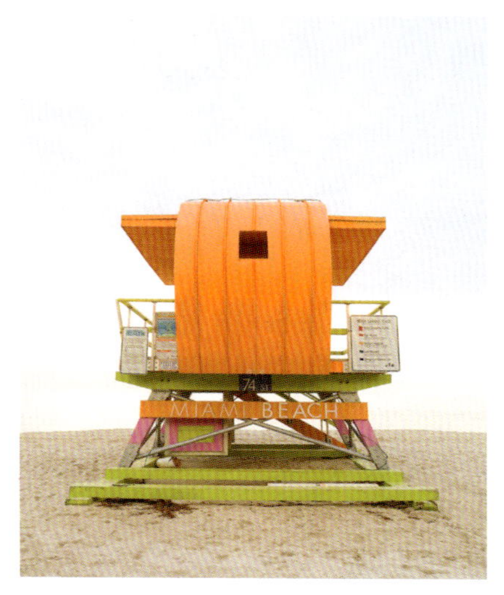

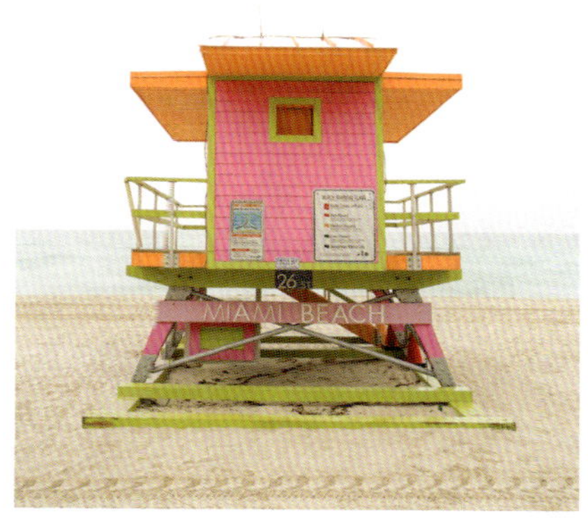

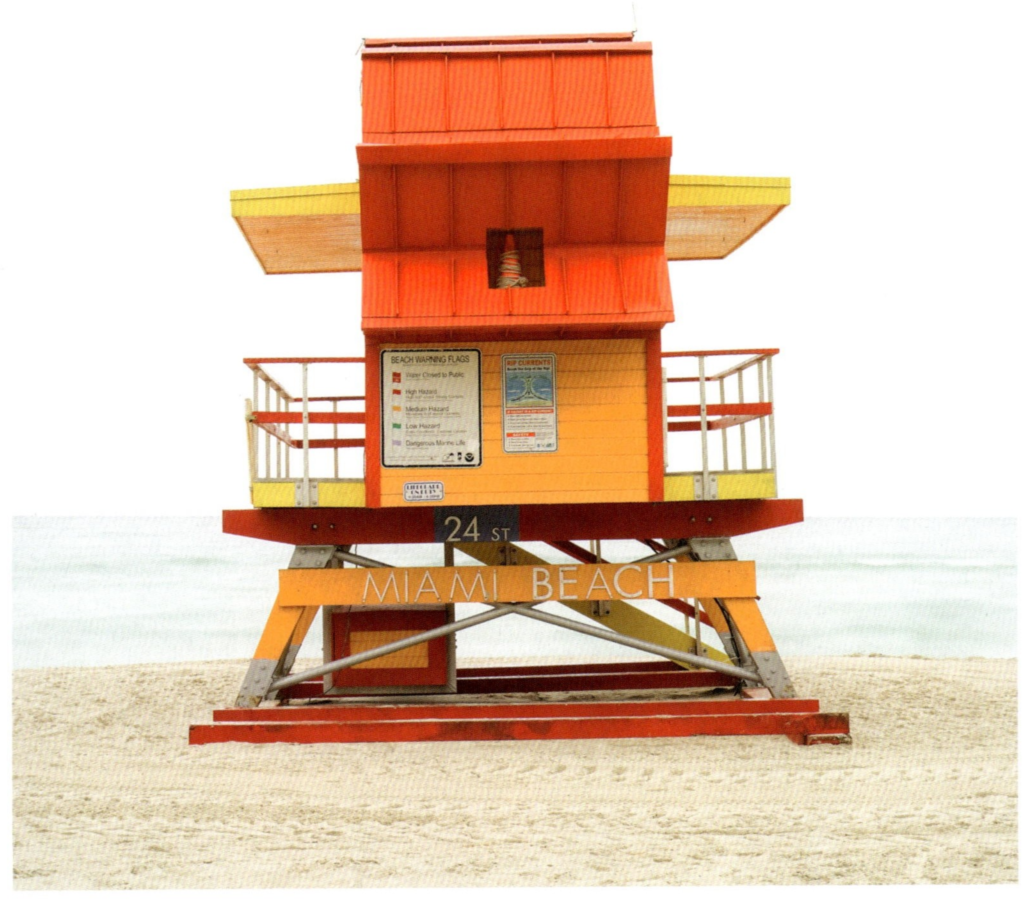

BEACH WARNING FLAGS
Water Closed to Public
High Hazard
Medium Hazard
Low Hazard
Dangerous Marine Life
RIP CURRENTS
Break the Grip of the Rip!
24 ST
MIAMI BEACH

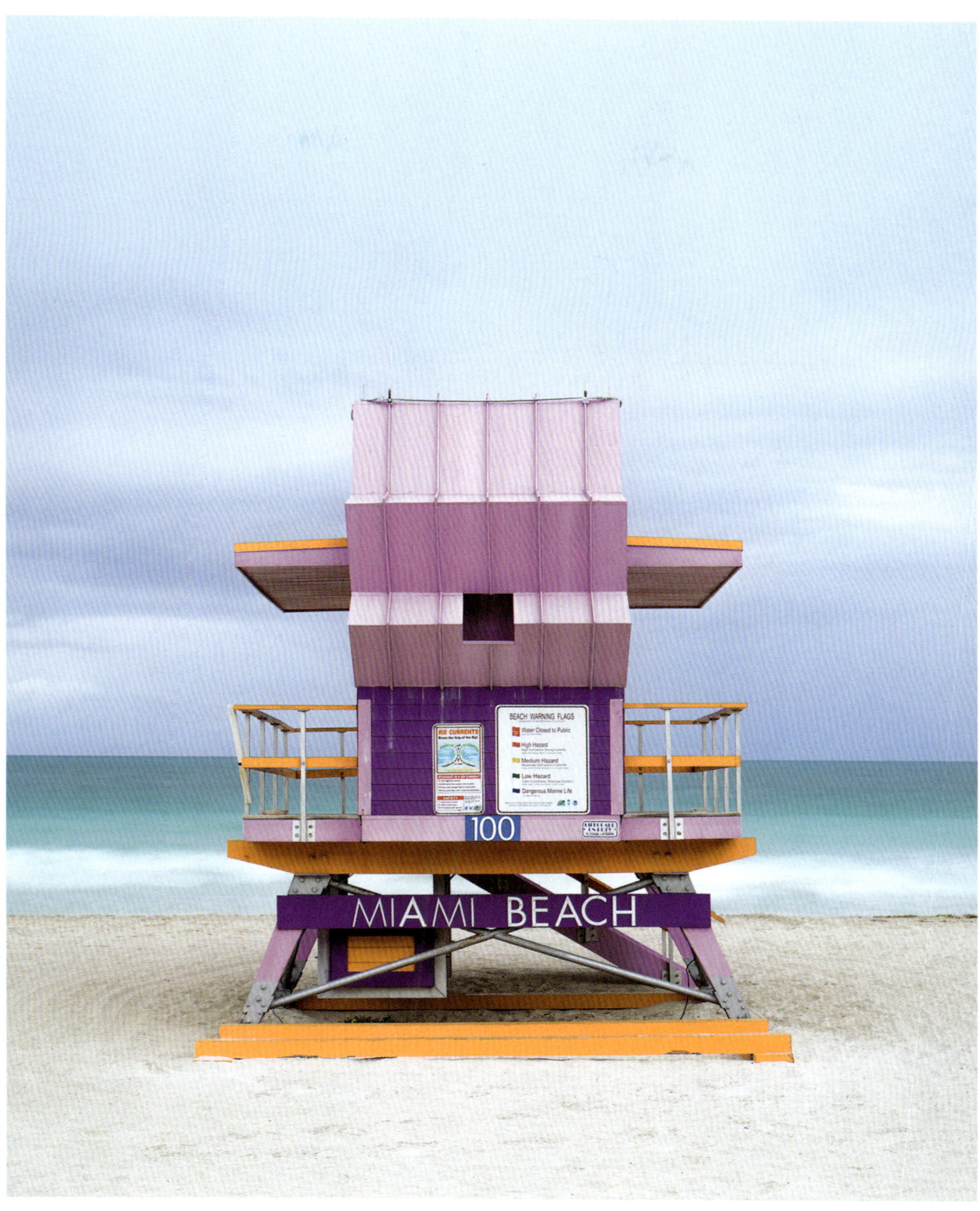

RIP CURRENTS
Break the Grip of the Rip!
BEACH WARNING FLAGS
Water Closed to Public
High Hazard
Medium Hazard
Low Hazard
Dangerous Marine Life
100
MIAMI BEACH

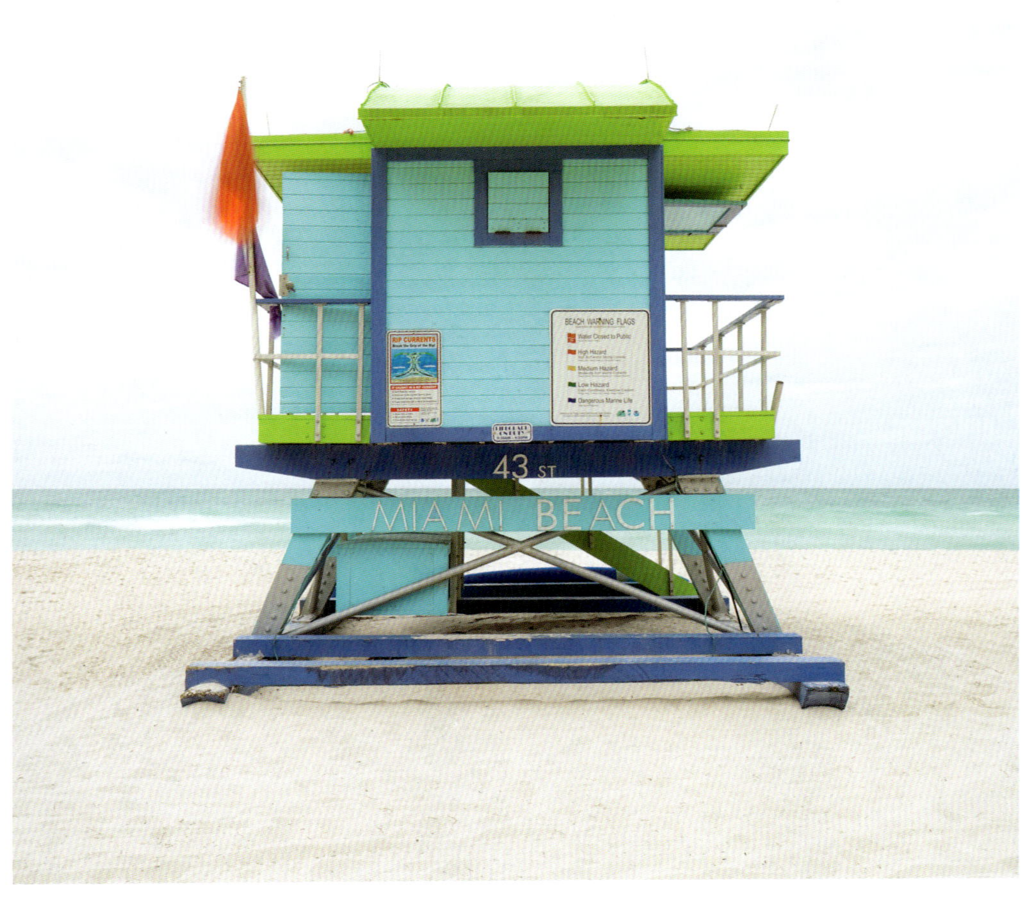
43 ST
MIAMI BEACH
RIP CURRENTS
BEACH WARNING FLAGS
Water Closed to Public
High Hazard
Medium Hazard
Low Hazard
Dangerous Marine Life

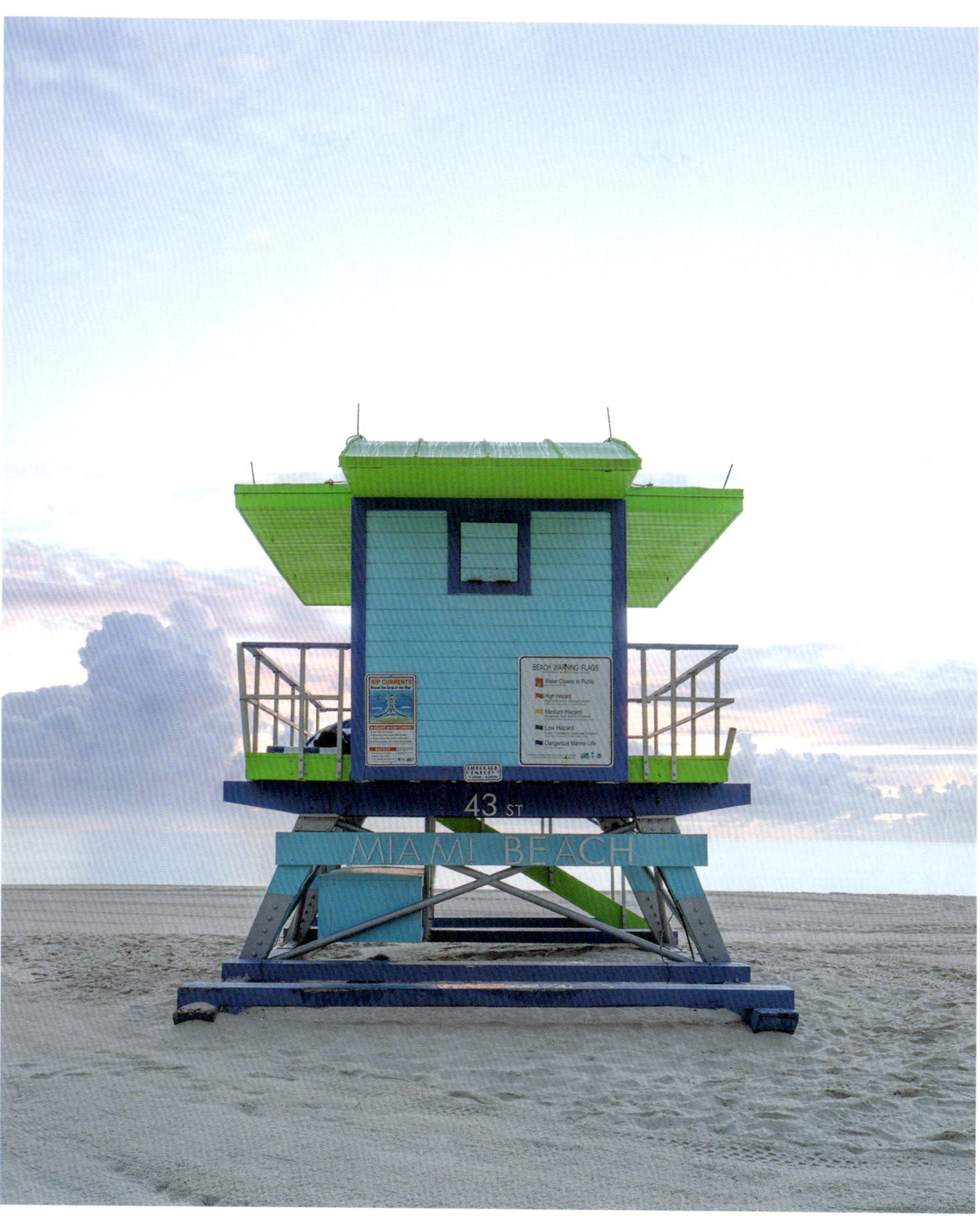
RIP CURRENTS
BEACH WARNING FLAGS
Water Closed to Public
High Hazard
Medium Hazard
Low Hazard
Dangerous Marine Life
43 ST
MIAMI BEACH

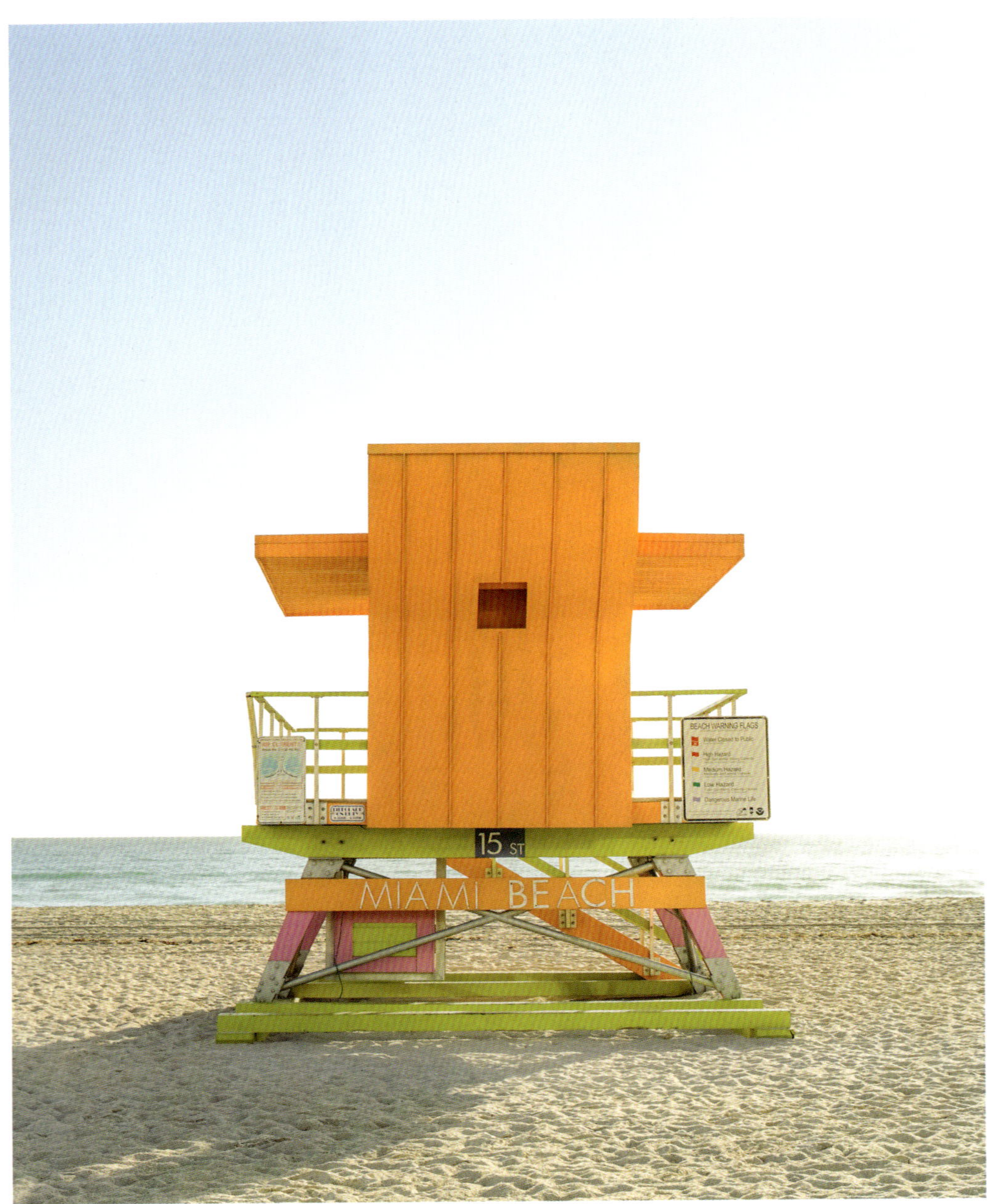
BEACH WARNING FLAGS
15 ST
MIAMI BEACH

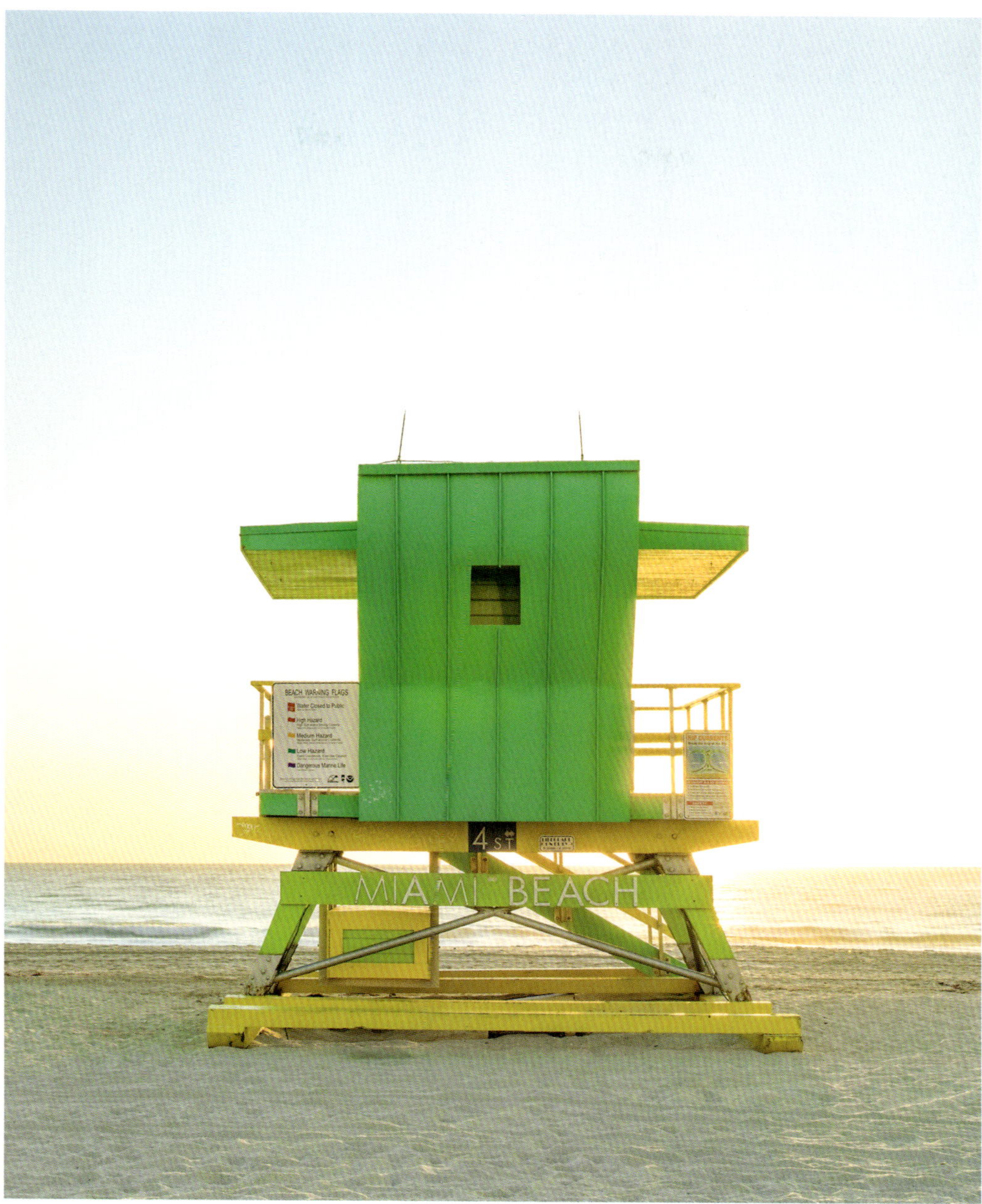

BEACH WARNING FLAGS
Water Closed to Public
High Hazard
Medium Hazard
Low Hazard
Dangerous Marine Life
4 ST
MIAMI BEACH

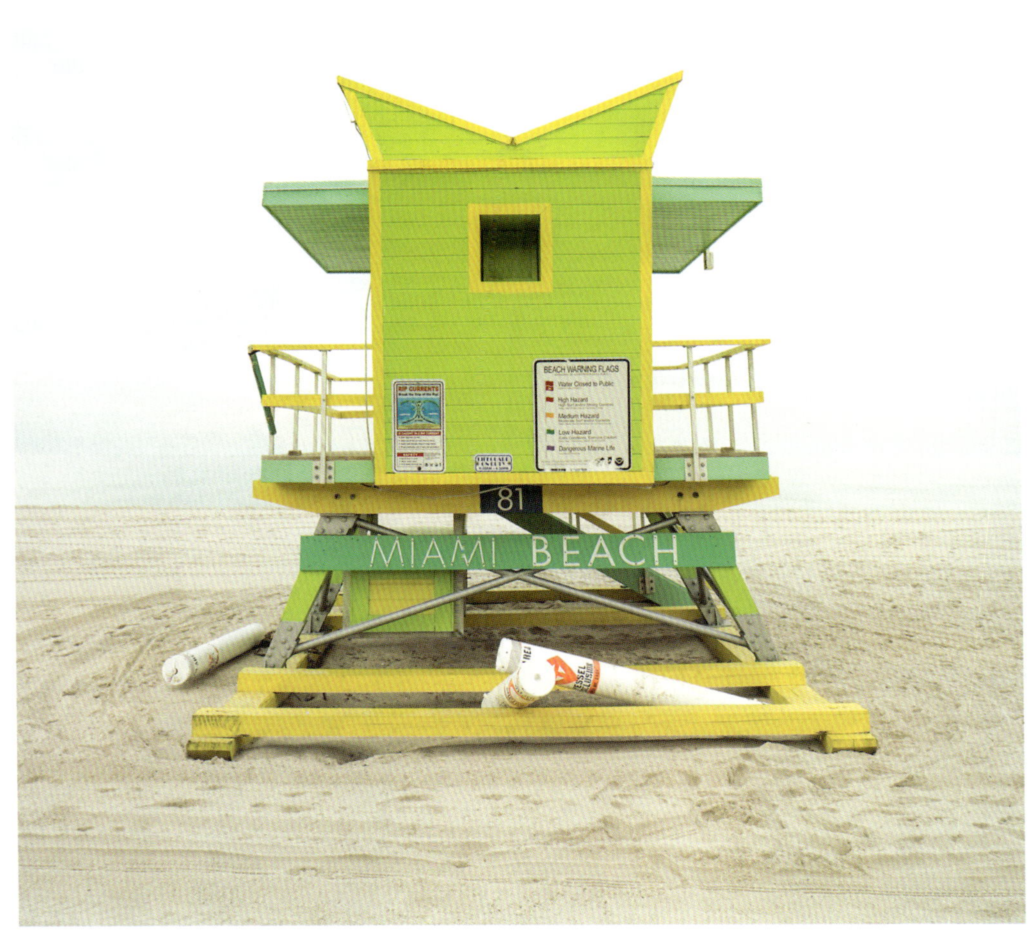
BEACH WARNING FLAGS
Water Closed to Public
High Hazard
Medium Hazard
Low Hazard
Dangerous Marine Life
RIP CURRENTS
81
MIAMI BEACH

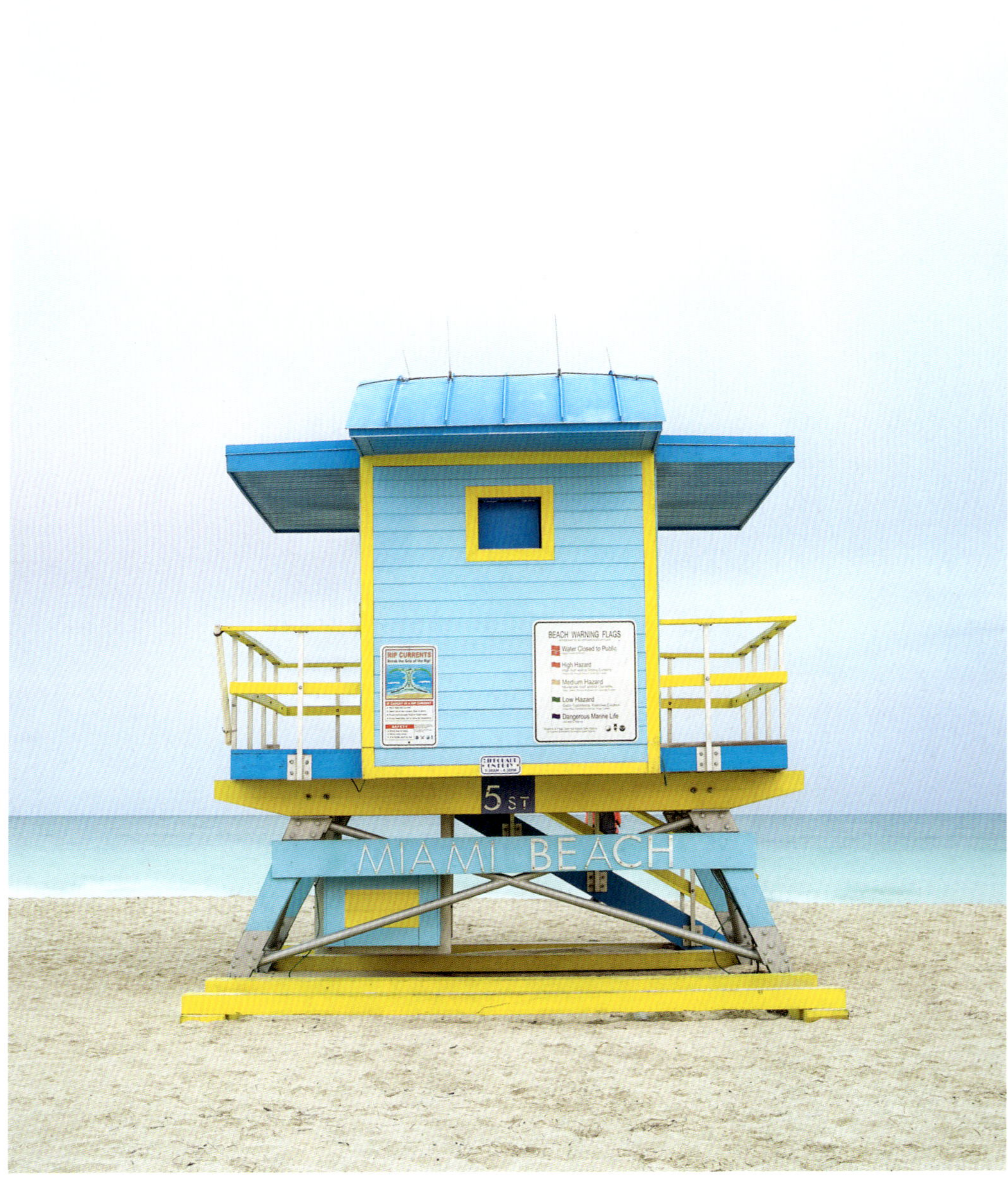
RIP CURRENTS
Break the Grip of the Rip!
BEACH WARNING FLAGS
Water Closed to Public
High Hazard
Medium Hazard
Low Hazard
Dangerous Marine Life
5 ST
MIAMI BEACH

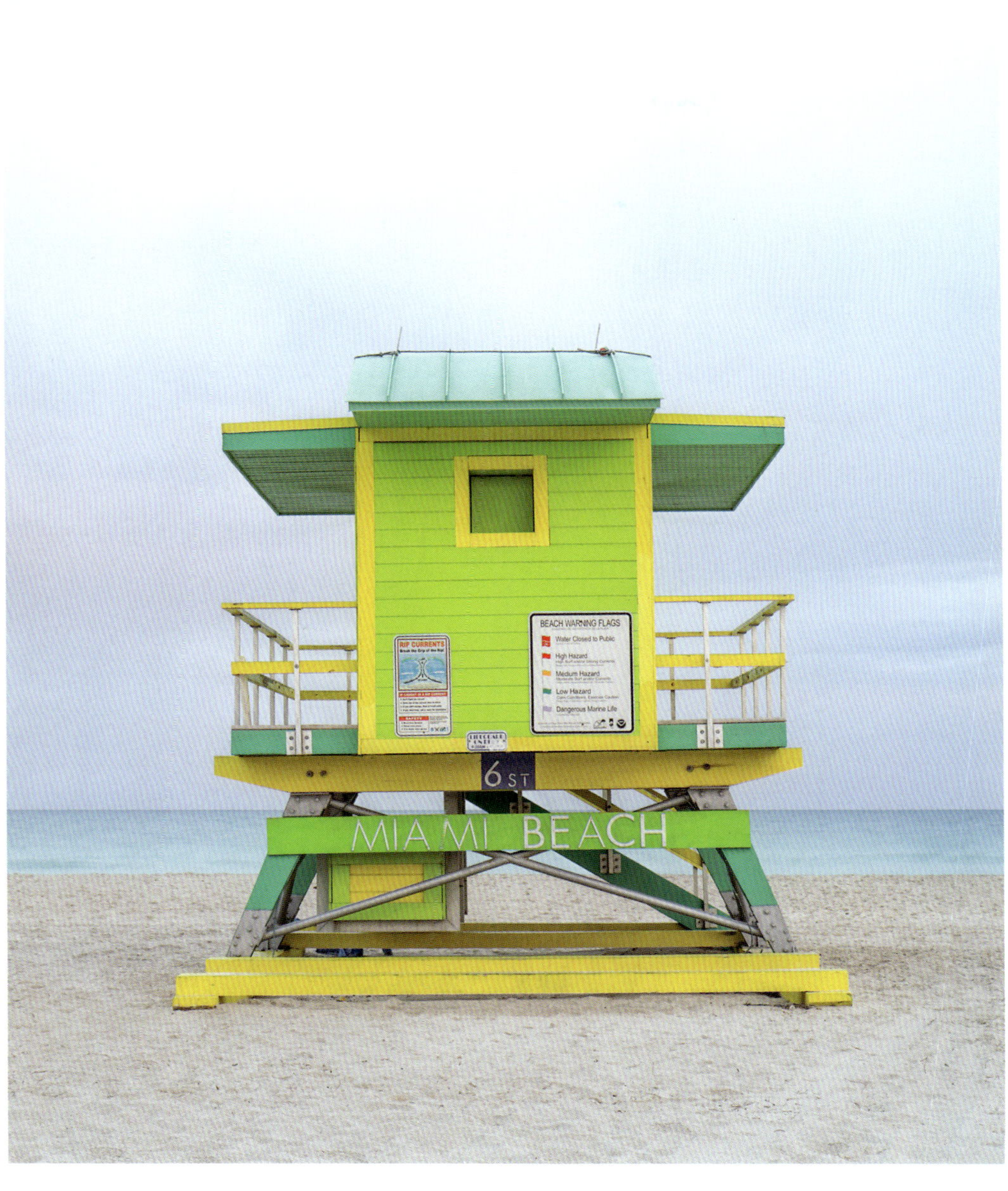
RIP CURRENTS
Break the Grip of the Rip!
BEACH WARNING FLAGS
Water Closed to Public
High Hazard
Medium Hazard
Low Hazard
Dangerous Marine Life
6 ST
MIAMI BEACH

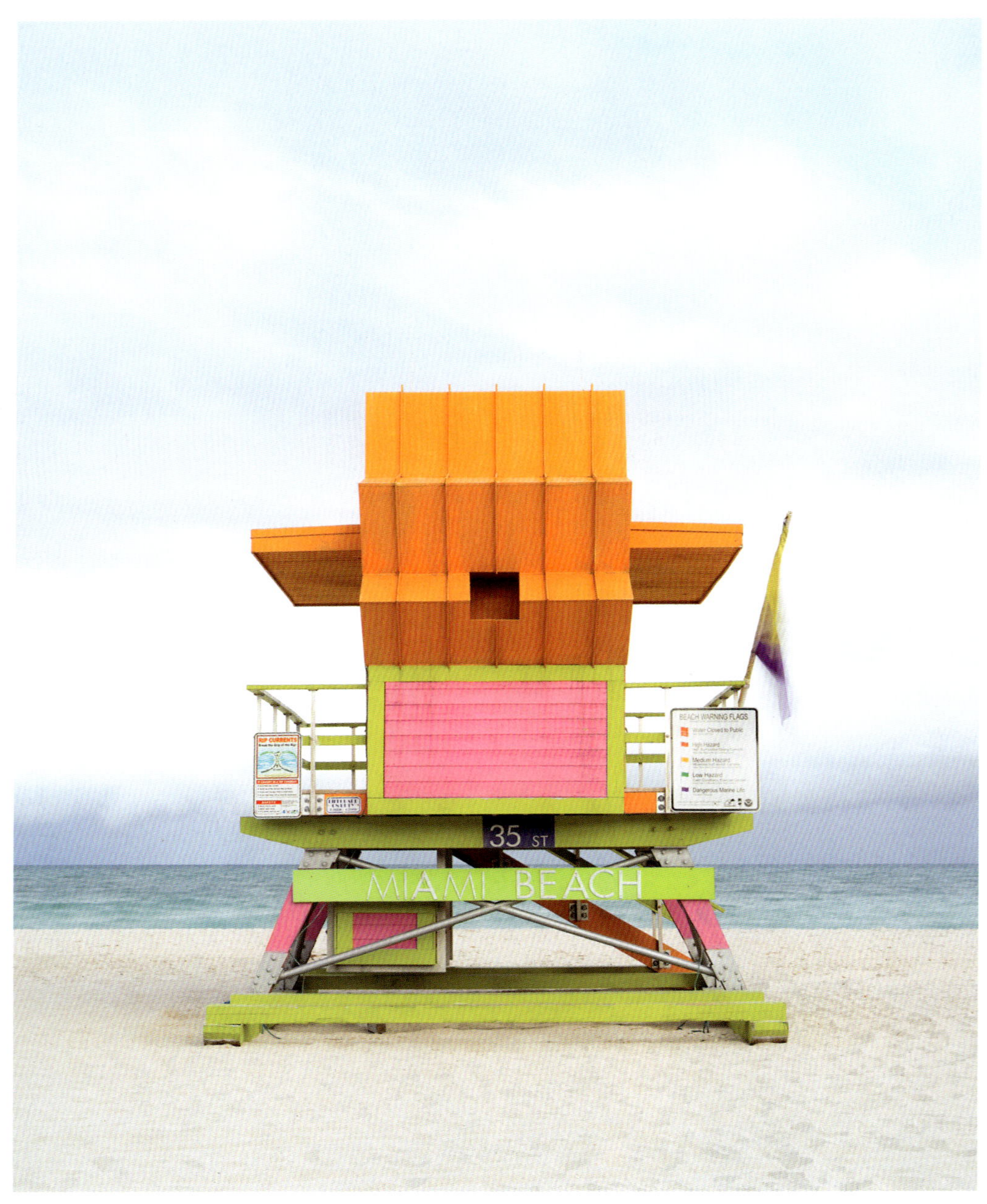
MIAMI BEACH
35 ST
BEACH WARNING FLAGS
RIP CURRENTS

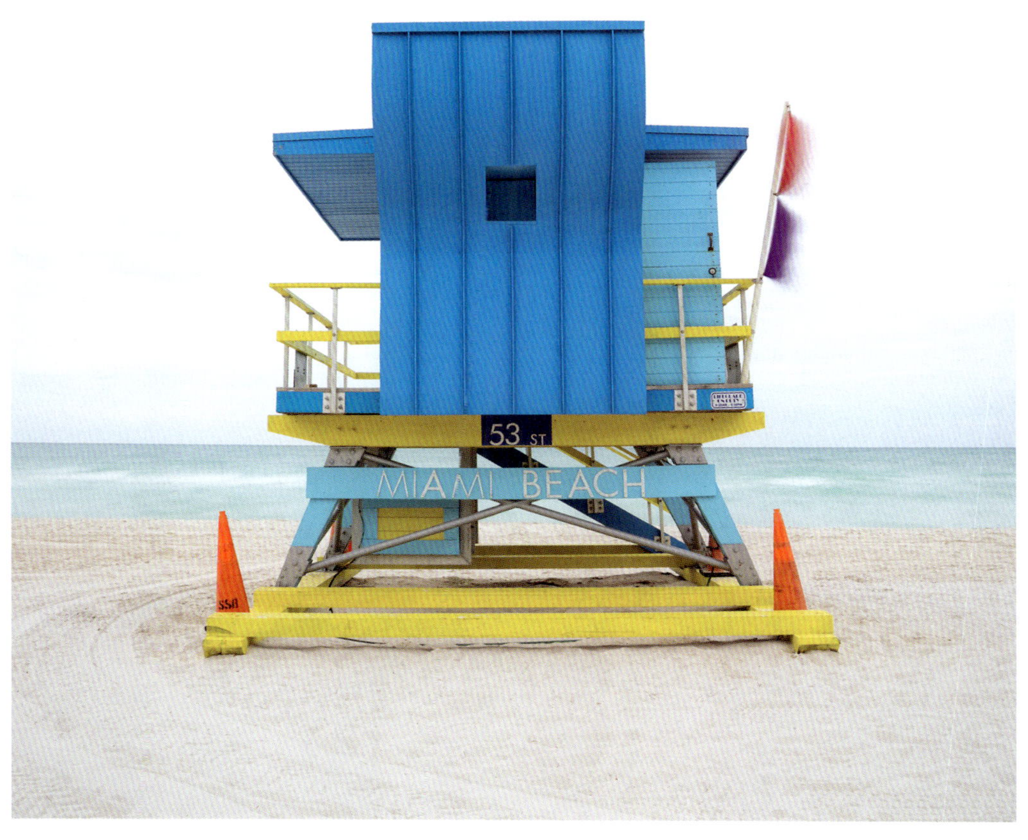
53 ST
MIAMI BEACH

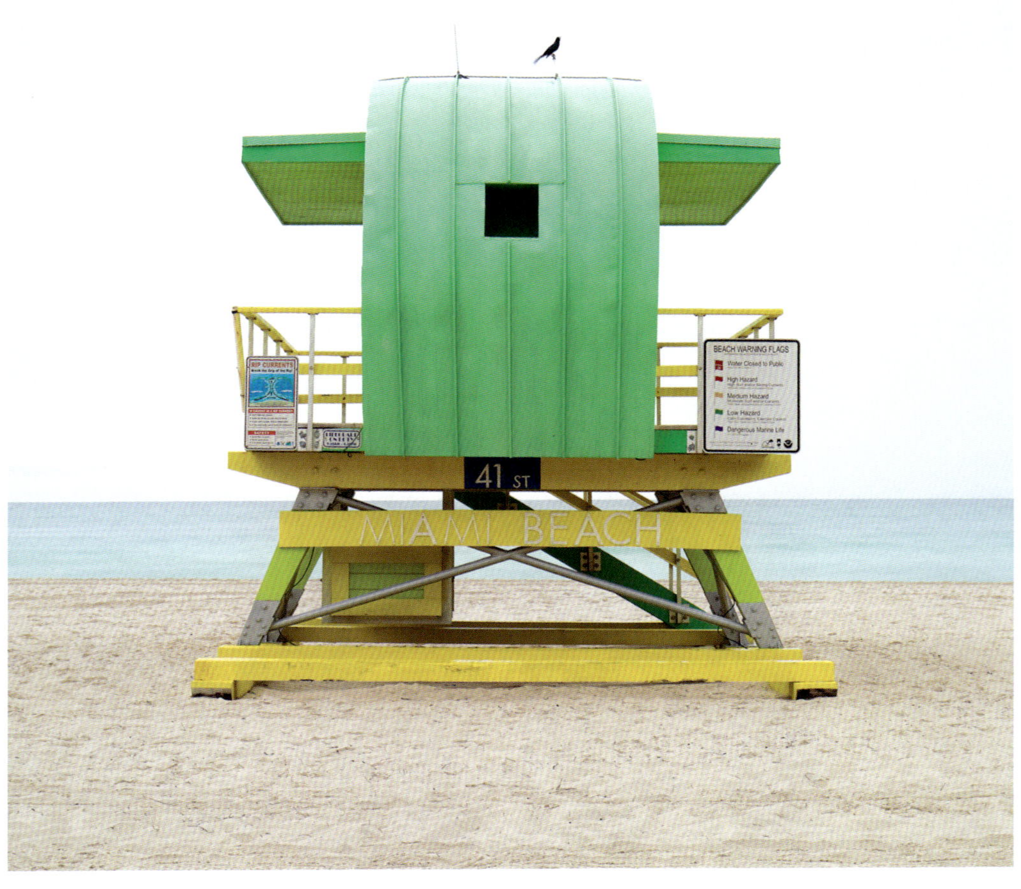
RIP CURRENTS
Break the Grip of the Rip!
BEACH WARNING FLAGS
Water Closed to Public
High Hazard
Medium Hazard
Low Hazard
Dangerous Marine Life
41 ST
MIAMI BEACH

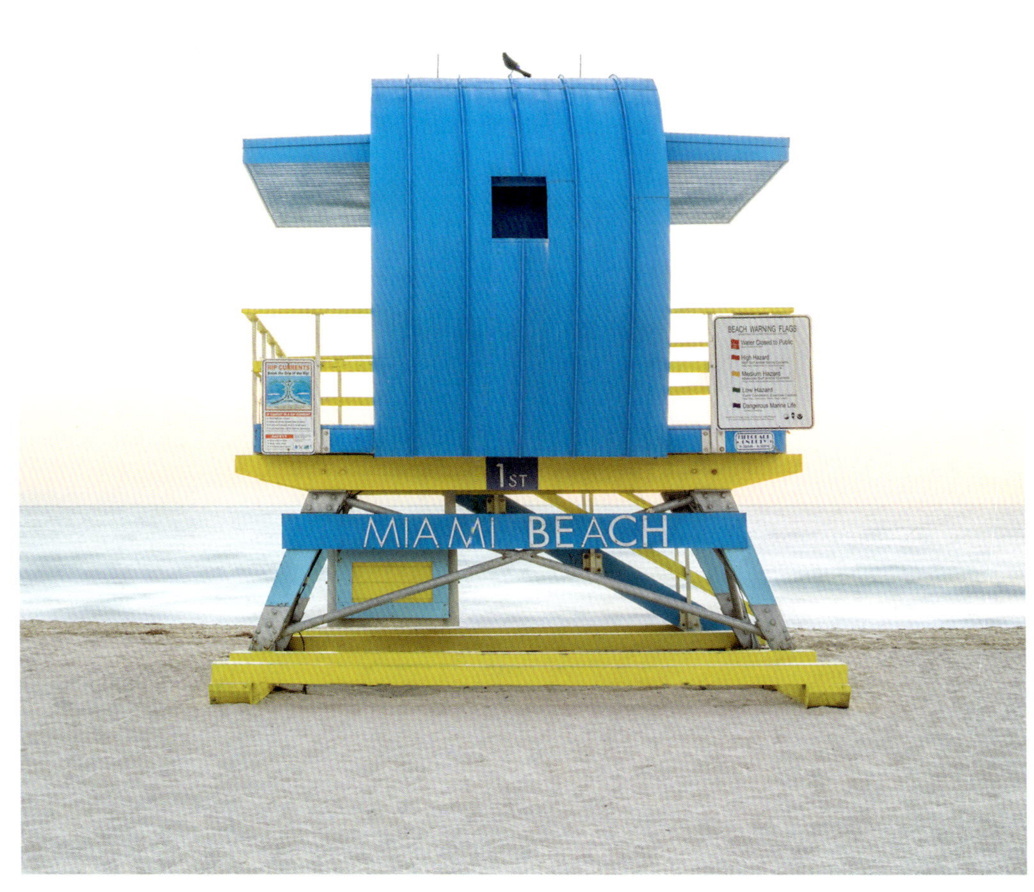
RIP CURRENTS
Break the Grip of the Rip!
BEACH WARNING FLAGS
Water Closed to Public
High Hazard
Medium Hazard
Low Hazard
Dangerous Marine Life
1ST
MIAMI BEACH

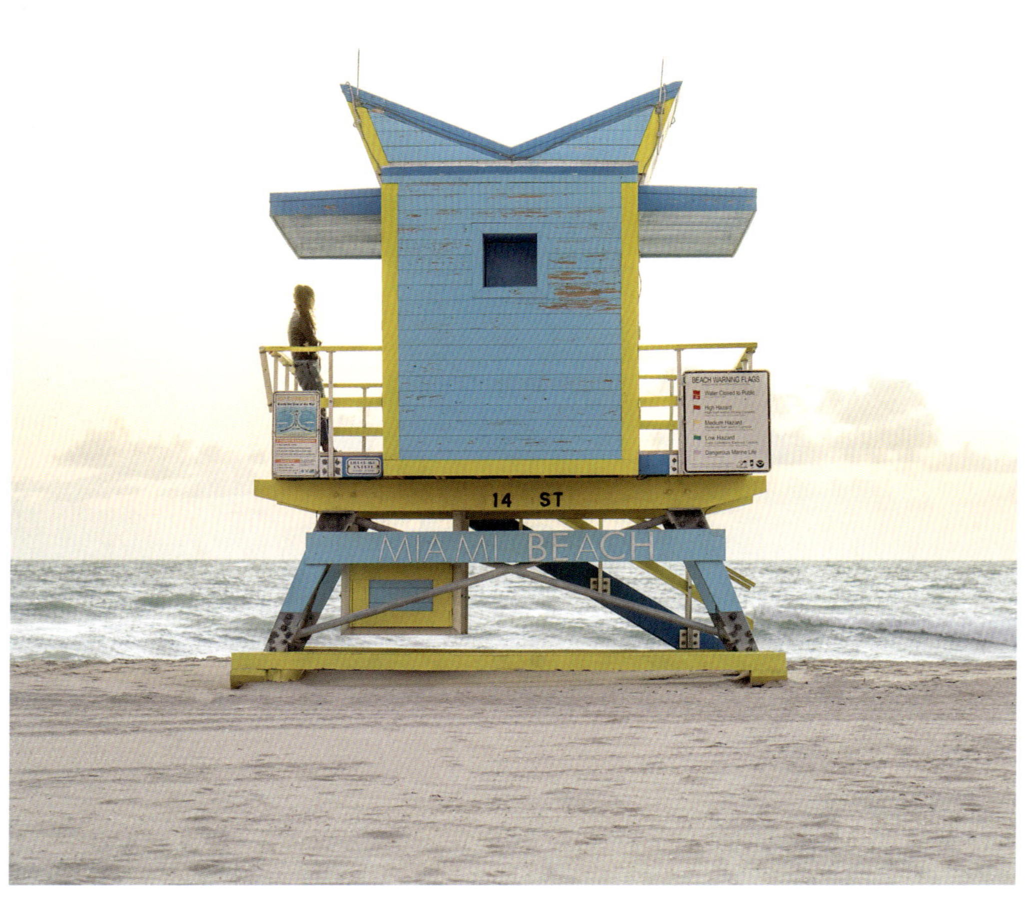
BEACH WARNING FLAGS
Water Closed to Public
High Hazard
Medium Hazard
Low Hazard
Dangerous Marine Life
14  ST
MIAMI BEACH

# INDEX

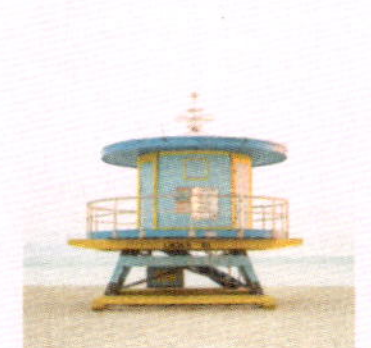

Lincoln Road

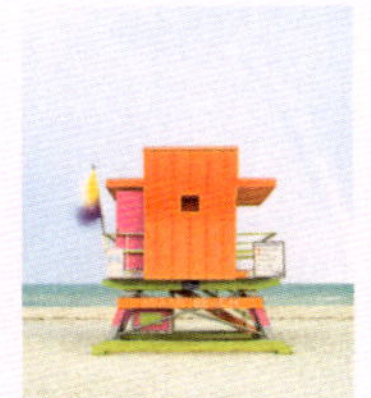

15th Street

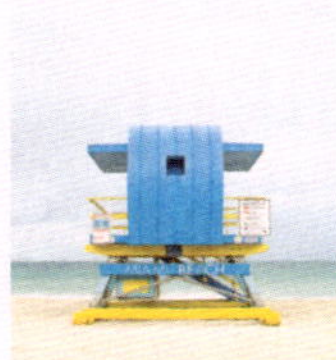

1st Street I

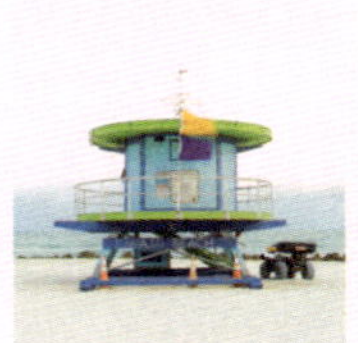

30th Street

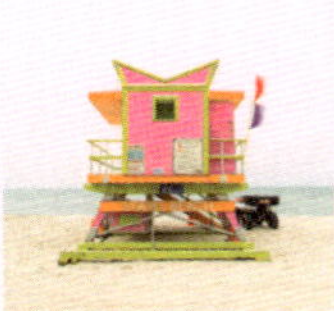

46th Street

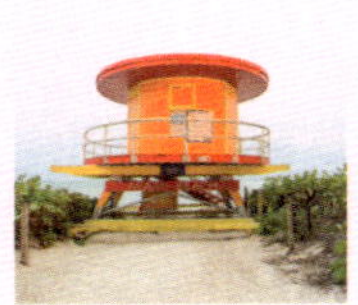

69th Street

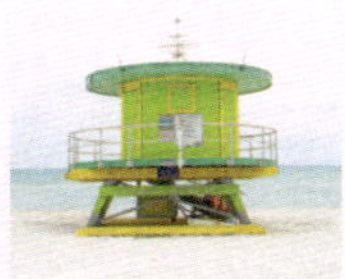

57th Street

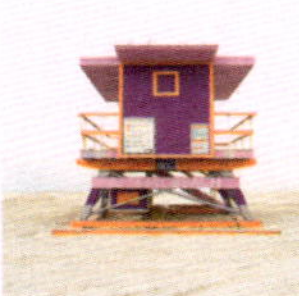

80th Street

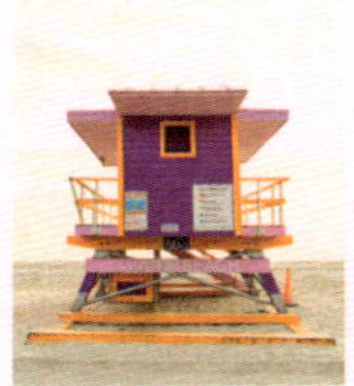

50th Street

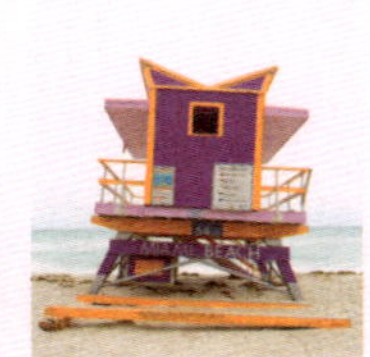

64th Street

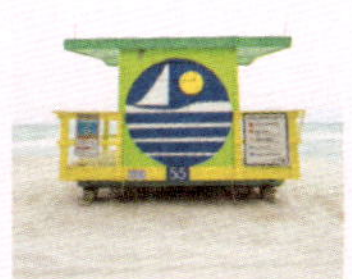

55th Street

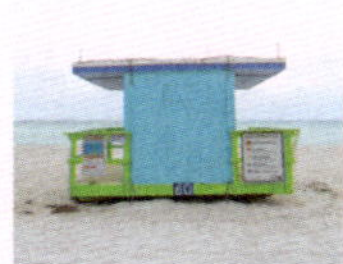

60th Street

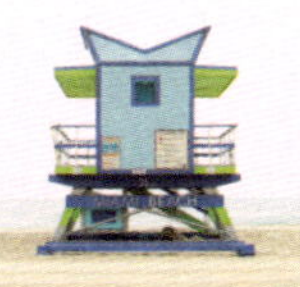

21st Street

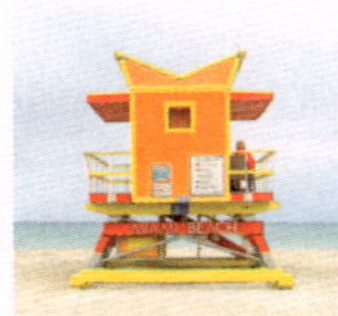

3rd Street I

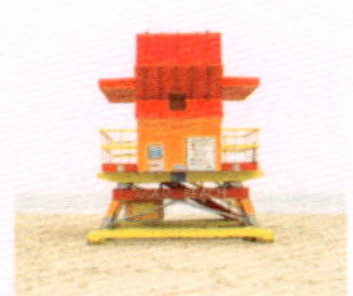

8th Street

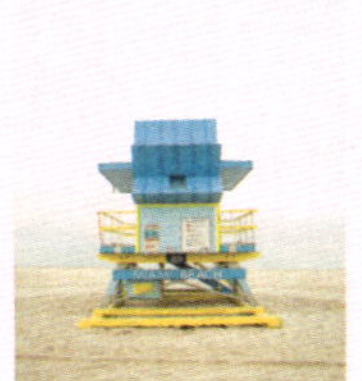

85th Street

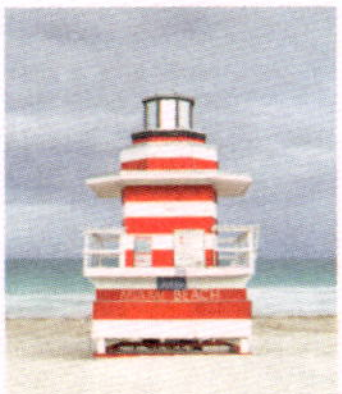

Jetty

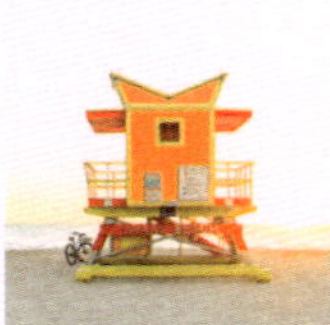

3rd Street II

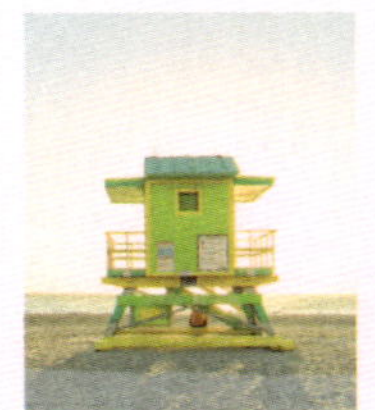

6th Street I

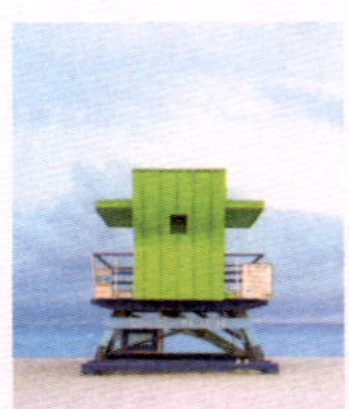

18th Street

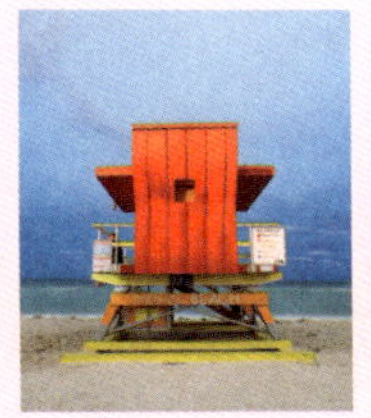

77th Street

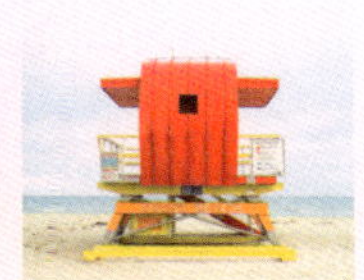

13th Street

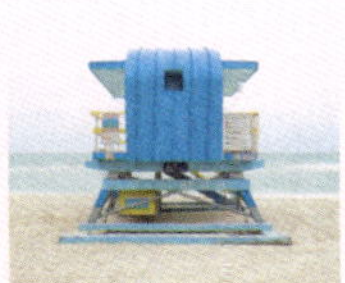

67th Street

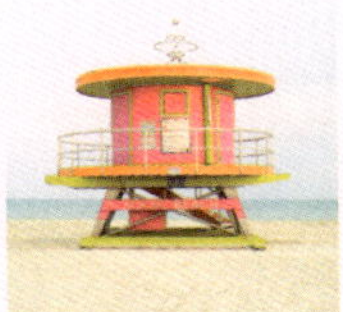

10th Street

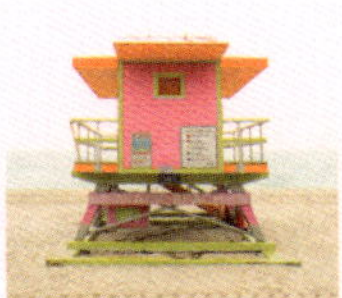

26th Street

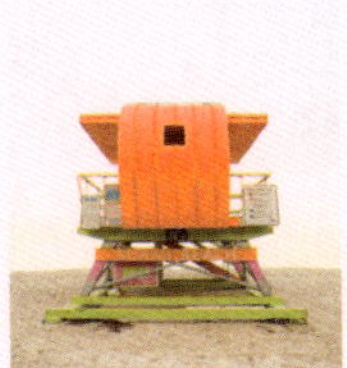

74th Street

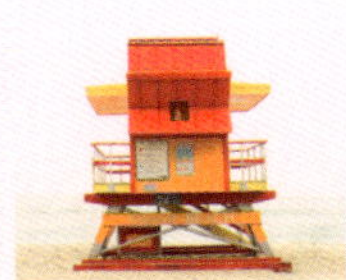

24th Street

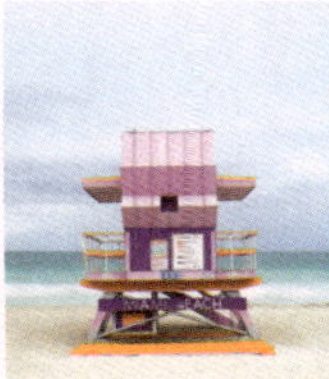

100

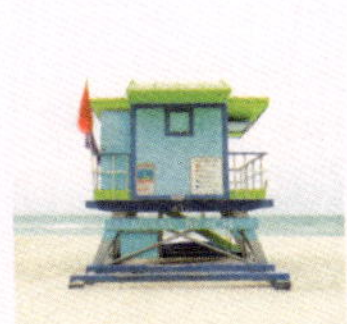

43rd Street I

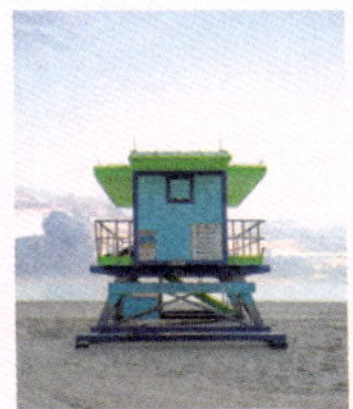

43rd Street II

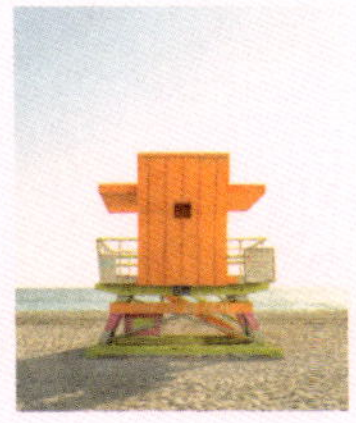

15th Street

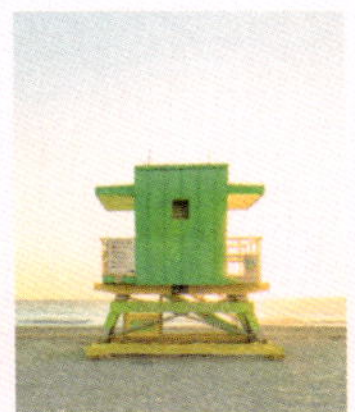

4th Street

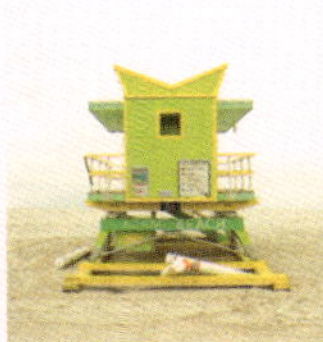

81st Street

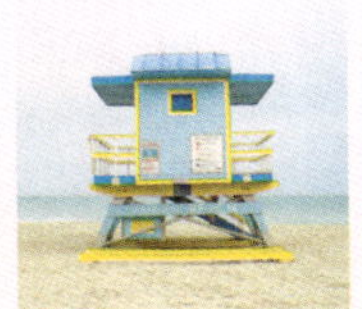

5th Street

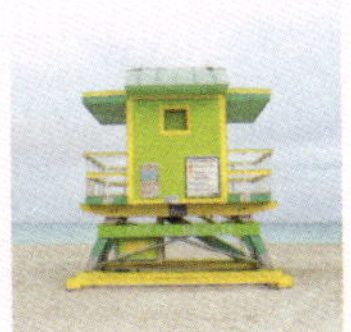

6th Street II

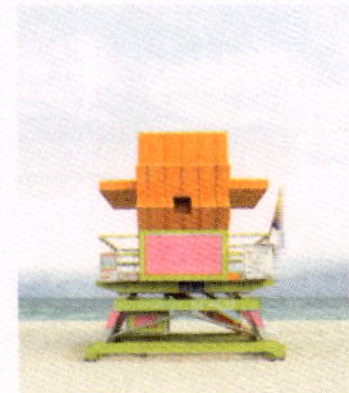

35th Street

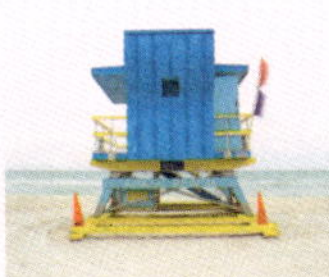

53rd Street

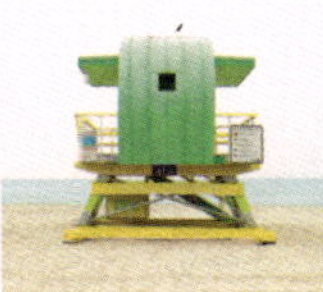

41st Street

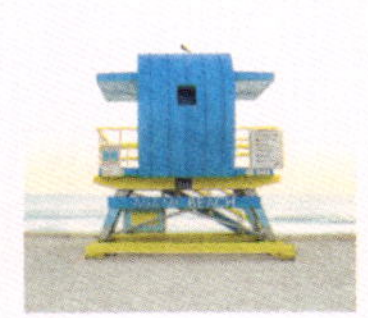

1st Street II

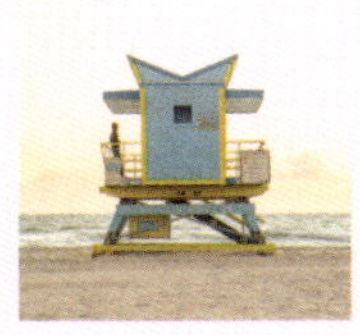

14th Street

Tommy Kwak is an award-winning American fine art photographer represented by Clic Gallery. His work has been exhibited internationally and is included in the private collection of Louis Vuitton at their locations in Manhattan, Seattle, and Cologne, Germany. Tommy grew up outside of Chicago, lived and worked in Brooklyn, NY for 13 years, and now resides in Montclair, NJ with his wife and daughter.

www.tommykwak.com

Karen Taylor Quinn is an editor based in Brooklyn, NY.
Since 2019, she has served as the Director of Social Media
at The New Yorker, leading an award-winning team of
journalists. Before moving to New York, she lived for 10 years
in Seattle, where she worked in magazines and food.

www.karentaylorquinn.com

For my wife Talea and daughter Emmy,
sisters Suzanne and Christina,
and for my mom Sarah.

All images © 2022 Tommy Kwak
This publication © 2022 Blurring Books

All rights reserved. No part of this publication may be reproduced, distributed, or transmitted in any form or by any means, or stored in a database or retrieval system, without the prior written permission of the publisher.

ISBN: 978-1-7361562-2-3

**Blurring Books**

Brooklyn, NY
www.blurringbooks.com | @blurringbooksnyc

Library of Congress Control Number: 2022905896

First published 2022. Fourth printing 2025.

Printed in China

Design: Tommy Kwak

Special thanks to: Db Burkeman and Costanza Prandoni at Blurring Books, Christiane Celle and the staff at Clic Gallery, Karen Taylor Quinn, Daria Pletneva, Julien Roubinet, Creative Capital, Skoll Foundation, and all the supporters on Kickstarter who made this book possible.

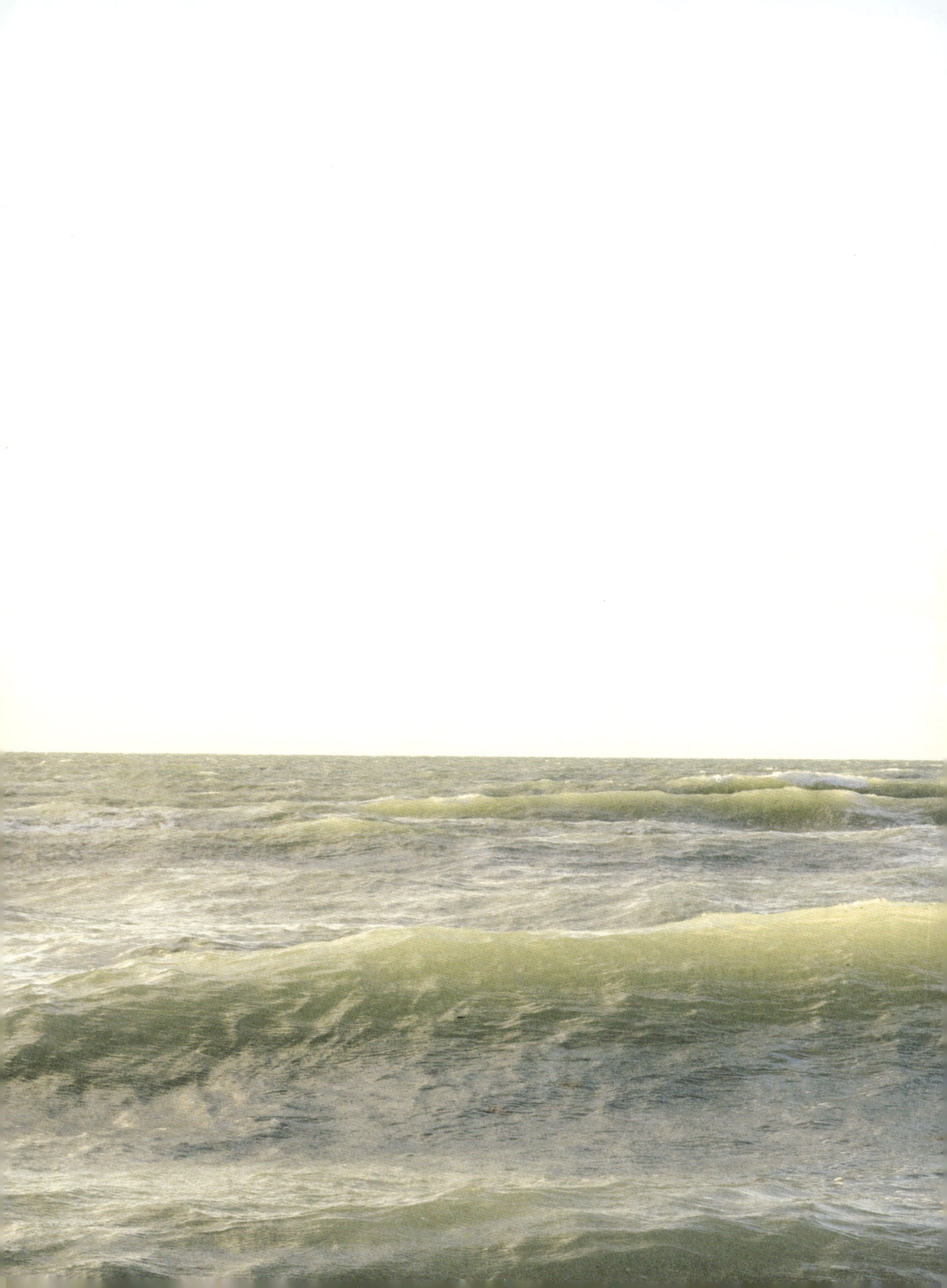

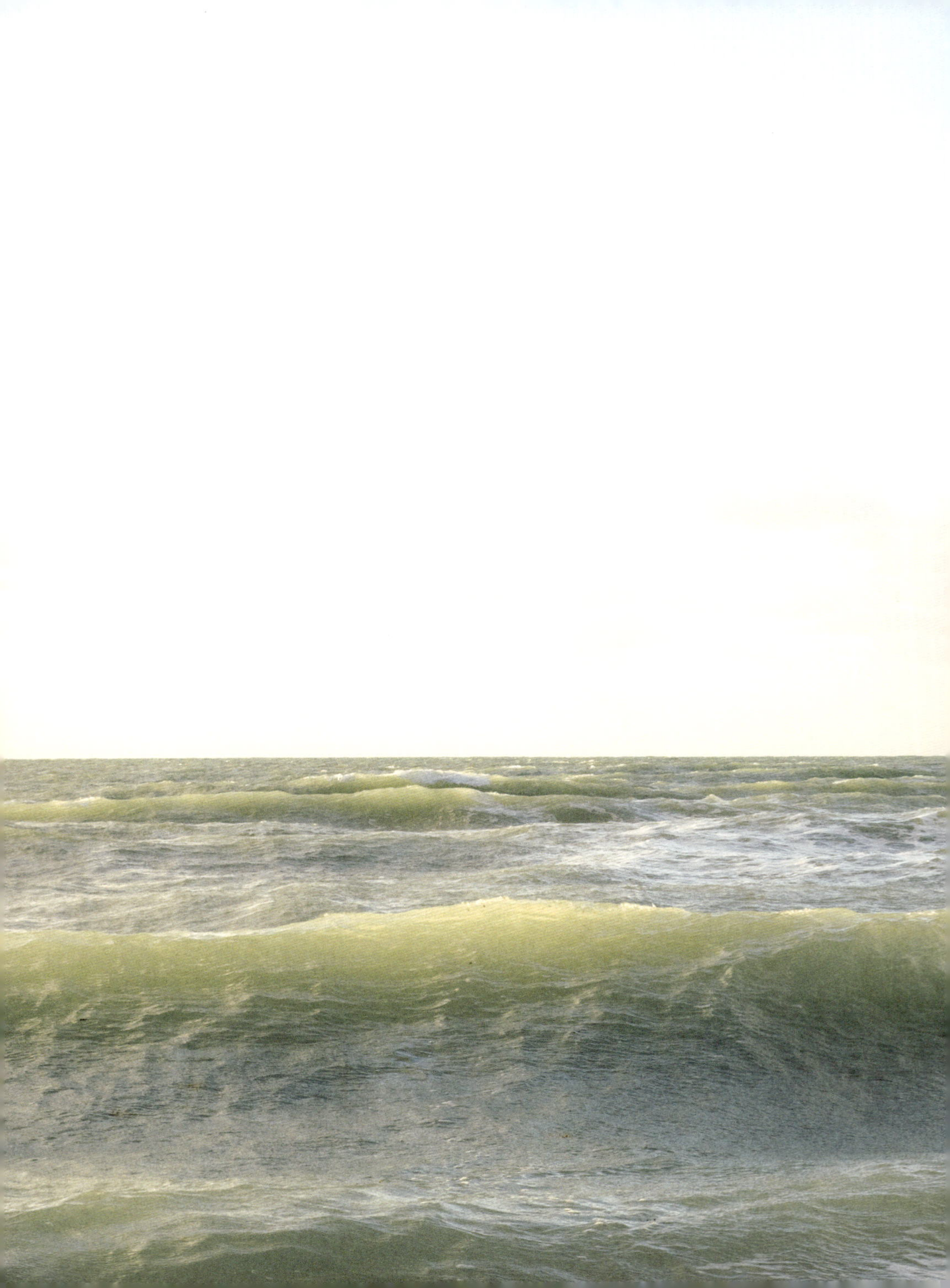